THE BREAK EQUATION

THE BREAK EQUATION

*It's not **what** life deals you, it's **how** you deal with life*

Copyright © 2011 by Mike Petriella

All rights reserved. No part of this book may be used or reproduced in any manner whatsoever without prior written consent of the author, except as provided by the United States of America copyright law.

Published by Advantage, Charleston, South Carolina.
Member of Advantage Media Group.

ADVANTAGE is a registered trademark and the Advantage colophon is a trademark of Advantage Media Group, Inc.

Printed in the United States of America.

ISBN: 978-1-59932-272-8
LCCN: 2011912565

This publication is designed to provide accurate and authoritative information in regard to the subject matter covered. It is sold with the understanding that the publisher is not engaged in rendering legal, accounting, or other professional services. If legal advice or other expert assistance is required, the services of a competent professional person should be sought.

Advantage Media Group is proud to be a part of the Tree Neutral® program. Tree Neutral offsets the number of trees consumed in the production and printing of this book by taking proactive steps such as planting trees in direct proportion to the number of trees used to print books. To learn more about Tree Neutral, please visit www.treeneutral.com. To learn more about Advantage's commitment to being a responsible steward of the environment, please visit www.advantagefamily.com/green

Advantage Media Group is a leading publisher of business, motivation, and self-help authors. Do you have a manuscript or book idea that you would like to have considered for publication? Please visit www.amgbook.com or call **1.866.775.1696**

*To my grandfather, Charles,
for the many breaks he gave to our family in life
— and while playing checkers.*

CONTENTS

Preface
What is The Break Equation?   9

Chapter 1:
Dare to Dream   13

Chapter 2:
Beyond the Glass Ceiling   21

Chapter 3:
Red Wine Wishes   35

Chapter 4:
Formula for Fulfillment   57

Chapter 5:
Know Thyself   69

Chapter 6:
Give Yourself a Break   77

Chapter 7:
A Tap on the Shoulder   93

Conclusion:
Now Is Your Moment   103

Appendix:
About The Break Equation Website   105

PREFACE

WHAT IS THE BREAK EQUATION?

The simplest things in life can often be hardest to see – and yet they can change your life when you finally get the picture. That's the case with *The Break Equation*.

This book will introduce you to a new way of understanding yourself and evaluating how people and events have influenced you. It can motivate you to pursue your passions and dreams – to understand that anything is possible when you set your heart and mind to it.

If you were to assign a numeric value to each good break that you have had in life and, likewise, each heartbreak, how would you score them? *The Break Equation* will present you with the opportunity to evaluate your life, to consider how you feel about the pluses and minuses, and calculate them – and after the equal sign will be you, the person you are today as formed by these events and your reactions to them.

This book will walk you step-by-step through the Break Equation Analysis, a tool for you to evaluate those significant events in your life and determine what we call your Break Score. Once you know your Break Score, you will have a new perspective through which you can better evaluate how you deal with events in your life. And with that new perspective, you can renew your self-confidence and commitment to pursue your dreams.

As your Break Score is dependent on how you feel about the most significant events in your life at a specific moment, it will change from year to year, even day to day. However, what will not change is its ability to open your eyes to those unique factors that motivate you.

Have you noticed that when you are around certain people, you begin to think big and daydream? And others seem to stifle you? By knowing your Break Score, you will begin to understand why that is so and be able to surround yourself with those who complement your ambitions and attitudes while managing those who may not.

The chapters to follow will guide you through the meaning of *The Break Equation,* the history of how it was created, and outline not only how to take the Break Equation Analysis on our website (www.TheBreakEquation.com) but also, and most importantly, what you can learn from it. You will learn of my personal journey and of several people that I have known who have taught me some important lessons through their breaks in life, both good and bad. We call their stories Breaking Profiles. We hope that the tools, people, and stories that you will encounter in the chapters ahead will become a positive break in your own life – and a call to action.

What is that business idea that you are passionate about, the one that you have been waiting to pursue one day when you have more time, have more money, or feel more confident that you have all the skills you need to succeed? The reality is that there may never be the perfect moment. We all have certain skills and strengths that will help us to accomplish our dreams, but we may not have all that it takes. Few of us do and recognizing that we may need some help is a big positive break in itself. Most importantly, we all need encouragers, mentors and advisers, people who share our ambitions, keep our motivations strong, and remind us that there is no need to wait – that the moment is now.

We encourage you to visit the Break Equation Incubator at www.TheBreakEquation.com. It is made up of a team of people who have a passion for helping to bring ideas and dreams to reality, to help multiply the good that can come from one person giving him or herself a break and taking the call to action on their business idea. And we hope that person is you.

You can read more about the tools and resources available on our website in the appendix to this book, including information about how the Break Equation Incubator process works – and how to get started.

But the first step is reaching out to yourself. Who are you, and why do you approach life as you do? It's a fundamental question, and many of us may not truly know the answer – yet how we react to events usually is more important than the events themselves. In essence, this book is about finding those unique factors that motivate you, identifying who you are at this moment in time, and understanding how life events that you have experienced may be influencing your confidence and perspective today.

By now, you have already invested ten minutes in reading the first few pages of *The Break Equation* for a reason. You are most likely seeking some change in your life. We hope *The Break Equation* is a spark that motivates you to overcome a previous challenge or mistake. We hope it reassures you that your dreams are leading you down the right path. We hope it reminds you that you do control your destiny and that anything is possible. We hope it inspires you to boldly step into the next chapter of your life, to find others in the world around you who have a common mission, and to reignite that passion you once had to make your mark on the world.

The Break Equation is a new perspective on the reality that we are all products of the events that have happened to us, good or bad. Some experiences add to our joys and ambitions, others subtract from them, some are negative and divisive – and some are so profoundly positive that they multiply through the years in a ripple effect. Such is the human equation, and each of us reacts uniquely to these experiences.

We often hear about others who live half way around the world from us, yet share common experiences. Generations before us shared many similar events and experiences – and our great grandchildren will, as well. What we are going through is certainly personal, but in most cases, is probably not unique. If we were to compare the most significant life events identified by millions of people, many would likely be the same – yet their Break Scores would vary greatly.

If our experiences are so similar, how do we end up so differently? The answer is a principle of *The Break Equation:* It is the way we react to events that most influences how our futures unfold. It's not what life deals you, it's how you deal with life.

CHAPTER 1:

DARE TO DREAM

Samantha will never forget that telephone call. It came at 10 a.m. on the day before she was to be married. Decades later, she still can feel the sting of her tears that morning. She remembers it all so vividly – and she smiles to think of it.

Samantha grew up as the oldest daughter of a modest family in a Colorado town. Her father ran a grocery store. Up before dawn, he didn't come home till dark. Her parents divorced when she was 12 – she learned later in life that her father had an affair with his young accountant.

Her father moved to Cleveland, Ohio after the divorce, and though she sometimes was shuttled off for visits, she couldn't regain trust in him. Samantha's mother did her best to raise her and her two brothers, but the children would often vividly recall the harsh words and anguish of those days and their mother's long months of weeping. The siblings and their mom developed a close bond as they made their way together into an uncertain future – and, in time, life did brighten for them all.

In her early teens, Samantha dreamed of running her own ski school, having fond memories of time spent with friends and family in the Colorado mountains. Despite her parents' divorce, Samantha dreamed of her own wedding day. She imagined her gown, the beautiful location, the music – and maybe even her father escorting her to the altar.

Samantha went to a local college and worked hard, studying business. After graduating, she began work at a ski shop in town, building a foundation for her dreams. She had a solid goal and was putting the pieces together to fulfill it.

That summer she met Matt, a good-looking and charismatic young man who lived not far away and had visited the ski shop with his friends. They struck up a conversation, exchanged numbers, and decided to meet for dinner. They dated, and she soon fell in love. Matt proposed fifteen months after the day they'd met, and they planned an April wedding.

They rented space at a local restaurant for a reception for up to a hundred people, sent out invitations, arranged the church ceremony, and made honeymoon plans. Samantha and her mother found just the right gown. All the name cards were ready. The date was fast approaching.

And then came that call. It was Matt. He was sorry. He gave no reason, but he couldn't go through with the wedding. His voice was flat.

She was devastated. Her head was spinning. How would she go on? What would she do?

What would you have done?

+   −   ×   ÷

You've heard it many times, no doubt, from a friend or relative: "That's it! I've reached my breaking point!" You may have shouted that yourself a time or two. Problems at work may seem insurmountable. Or a marriage is on the brink. At some pivotal moment, life's frustrations and exasperations or just the onslaught of responsibilities seem too much to bear.

Take heart. Your breaking point can be a defining moment. At such points, you stand at a crossroads: Do you give up, or do you persevere? Do you break down, or do you seize your break?

Through the perspective of time, we redefine the many breaks, good and bad, that each of us has in our lives. Those bad ones can seem good, in retrospect. Or we may come to rue the ones we once embraced so enthusiastically. It seems every silver lining has a cloud.

As we reflect on our lives, it's not hard to identify those times when we were called to take decisive action. Sometimes we faced issues that we needed to correct. But at other times, we were presented with opportunities that we could pursue – by taking action, we had a chance to fulfill a dream.

This book will help you identify those seminal moments in your life, your Break Factors, that have made you who you are today and make you think and react the way that you do. Knowledge is power, and by understanding what motivates you and what frustrates you, you will have a new lens through which to consider what to pursue and what to avoid – and which personality characteristics in others may bring out the best, or the worst, in you.

The Break Equation presents you with the opportunity to gain a new perspective on your life and the key moments you have experienced. You will gain insight to help guide your ambitions and realize that you have the power, in your own unique way, to give yourself a break.

If you have been frustrated, lost, or demotivated, you deserve to dream again. There is a passion inside you waiting to blossom, and there's no time like now to take the first steps. Sure, it may have been so long since you've let yourself dream that you scarcely know how or where to start. Far too often, ambitions fade from sheer frustration. Just remember this: You can talk about your dreams for the rest of your life. But they'll never come true unless you act.

Name your dream, however big or small: Perhaps it is to start a bed-and-breakfast, and you're a natural host and a great cook – but don't care much for bookkeeping. You can bet there are bookkeepers out there who would love to start a bed-and-breakfast – if only they knew how to cook. The size, value, and importance, of a dream is certainly a personal decision. What may seem like a trivial business pursuit to you may be a life-long passion to me, and vice-versa. We all have the right to define our own dreams and pursue them. The dream that earns the most money or fame is not the winner – the winner is he or she who finds fulfillment by achieving such a goal.

Through *The Break Equation,* you can see that events in your own life are not that different from the experiences of those around you, those who came before, or those who will follow. You can learn from this commonality. You just need to open your mind, see opportunities, and take action. Embrace the positive breaks and get a proper perspective on the negative ones – after all, an event lasts only for a moment, yet your reaction to it could last a lifetime if you allowed that.

Do you remember when your aspirations led you to believe anything was possible, that you could own that bed-and-breakfast? You can. It's time to take that next step. Think of *The Break Equation* as a dream incubator.

I'll give you all the details later, but for now – what became of poor Samantha?

$$+ \quad - \quad \times \quad \div$$

You might expect that Samantha went into a deep spiral of depression, seeing Matt's departure as a repeat of her father's abandonment. Rooted inside her was doubt about relationships, and those doubts, planted so many years earlier, now surfaced. She became cynical not only of men but also of most other relationships in her life. What her father had done and what Matt had done became her filter on the world, thwarting her spirit and her ambitions. Dreams faded. Why try, when others will fail you? She never opened that ski school.

You might expect that's what happened, because it's unfortunately a common story. We've all known a few souls like Samantha, stymied by sadness, blocked from their passions and dreams. Samantha is not a real person – rather, she is a composite of people you've no doubt known.

Rewind. Let's take Samantha back to that devastating telephone call and chart a new course for her. Yes, all those feelings surfaced: She felt anew the pain of her father's infidelity. She cried bitter tears. And when she stopped crying, she felt numb. She so badly needed a loving hand.

That very evening, when Samantha had hoped to be the shining bride-to-be and the center of attention, she and her mother talked. As her daughter spilled out her agony, her mom listened attentively. At first, her mother gazed out the window toward the snowy slopes, feeling again a pain she once knew. Then she looked deep into Samantha's eyes, smiling gently. They embraced.

Mother and daughter put a plan together. They had already spent thousands of dollars for the reception hall and meals for up to a hundred people, and they were not about to let it go to waste. They called a local shelter with invitations for a hundred people to join them the next day for several hours of warm fellowship and fine dining.

Out of pain is born the empathy and perspective that defines wisdom – a pain such as Samantha's mother had endured. And it was her mother who was there for her. At her worst moment, facing one of her life's biggest challenges, Samantha transformed her perspective. She could either define, or be defined.

Leaning upon her mother, Samantha turned her heartbreak into a life break. Devastation became motivation. She channeled her disappointment and anger into an act of community kindness, and the appreciation and good will that ensued gave her the momentum she needed.

Two years later, she opened her ski school, determined to succeed. She remained wary of men, but that evolved into a discriminating good taste and appreciation of good character. She eventually met a man whom she could admire – one whom, by comparison, made Matt appear to her in a very different, and less flattering, way from how she once felt. She wondered what she'd ever seen in him, and she now knew that the day he had called to bow out of the wedding was one of her life's best.

She and her mother often thought about those homeless strangers who had been their guests on a day that had been destined for sadness. One day, ten years later, Samantha's mother heard a radio interview with the director of the region's food banks. Once, he had been down and out himself – until one day, strangers had invited him to an unusual feast of lobster and steak and he began to wonder whether he, too, might have something, however humble, to share.

That's how it is with acts of charity and compassion: The goodwill spills into the future. Munificence multiplies.

Samantha's mom understood that. In her daughter's tears she saw a reflection of herself, years earlier, when she felt forsaken and alone. Samantha was lucky to have had her mother there for her, someone who could empathize with her hurting heart, someone who knew just what to do. The pain of the past became the blessing of today. Yes, her mother had a bad break once, and it became Samantha's good one.

Samantha had stood at her breaking point and stepped boldly forward, not into an abyss but onto the slopes leading to her mountaintop. She needed a guide, someone who had been there. Perhaps you, too, have been there, and want to show someone else how to find a break.

CHAPTER 2:

BEYOND THE GLASS CEILING

You've heard of the glass ceiling. It's what stifles careers and opportunities. It's not easy to see a glass ceiling, but if you're trying to climb the steps and your head crashes into one, you'll wince from the pain.

The glass ceiling might be that all-too-common one of age or gender or race or religion. It might be your weight or appearance. You may feel held back or trapped because your finances or education are limited. It can start to feel that you can rise only so far and no more.

Glass ceilings are unfortunate realities in the workplace – but they should never be able to stifle your passions. If your dreams endure, you will find a way. Think of your career that way – as your pursuit of what you feel passionate about. You may hit a glass ceiling in a job, but one job is only one small phase of your lifelong career. A career is not defined by any one job, or any one employer, or any one title you may carry.

When I was a student at Villanova University, I was the head RA (resident assistant) in an on-campus dorm housing a few hundred freshman students during my senior year. At the end of that year, we raised enough money to put a bench outside our dorm to commemorate the year of 1997 in Katherine Hall. We had a plaque mounted on the bench that said "Life is a journey, not a destination. Enjoy the ride." This philosophy I carry with me today as I travel the path of my career endeavors.

Your career is your journey, and it involves many stops along the way. Some will frustrate you, but no one is the final destination. Have you ever read a great book with a dull chapter or two? I've watched many a baseball game with a few boring innings. In fact, I've tracked the New York Yankees for many seasons during which they endured several tough weeks or months, yet went on to win the pennant. If you find yourself in a dull or frustrating job, that doesn't mean your career still can't be thrilling. It's a reminder to persevere.

Imagine yourself as a young administrative assistant of a well-known shipping company. After a couple of years there, you realize that what you'd truly love to be doing is marketing. So you tell your boss, who says she just can't spare someone with your experience when she has two new hires to train. "One more year, then maybe we can revisit the idea. Until then, we need you here," the boss says.

That one year passes, and then another. There always seems to be some reason, or some rule, that puts your goal just out of reach. The people you report to have a different plan for you. Your plans and ambitions simply don't fit into their plan at this time – and they hold you back, selfishly at times. You become so frustrated and worn down that you stop dreaming and you stop trying.

We all come across obstacles like that on the job and in life. It's our duty to ourselves, when that happens, to find a way around them. In the end, we always need to take responsibility for the direction of our lives. Think of it as a maze. You ran into a wall. You need to back up and figure out where to go next.

If you continually allow other people to hold you back or direct your life, pessimism may mount. You may feel empty, and it can carry over into your personal life. It can hurt a marriage and friendships. We turn to other, less productive ways to spend our time. It can lead to general depression. Yet we must all remember that this one bad job or glass ceiling doesn't mean your career is finished or forever diminished. It's just time to use this as a wake-up call to give yourself a new break in life.

Typically, a work week is about forty hours. At 9 a.m., we leave our home and family life and enter a new environment with its own rules, regulations, policies, and expectations. And what happens after 5 p.m.? We head back home to family – and take those regulations with us. They tend to guide us even for the 128 hours that remain in our 168-hour week.

Those forty hours, however, are only about a quarter of the time available to us in a week. But the limitations that we feel on the job often carry over to influence how we think, how we dream, how we feel about ourselves. We might truly want to grow, to succeed, to earn more – but our head hurts from hitting that glass ceiling at work and we feel unqualified. We wonder about the core reason we're being held back. At home, we likewise might feel unqualified, held back, wondering about our worth. In the pit of the stomach, dread builds. Going to work becomes a chore.

Now, ask yourself this: Do you try to be a good person only 25 percent of the time? Do you try to eat well only 25 percent of the time? Do you only hope to win in sports a quarter of the time? Do you want to be a good parent for several hours a day, but mostly not? Do you want to be happy only 25 percent of your life? Of course not!

Why, then, do we allow our ambitions, dreams, and self-confidence to be driven by limitations dictated by a workplace where we spend only a portion of our time?

Tomorrow, as you head home from work, try this: Look up before you step out of the doorway from the vestibule. What do you see? Most likely it's a ceiling a few feet over your head. Then step outside and look up again. Do you see the tops of trees rising to the heavens, birds chirping in the branches? Do you see the sun and blue sky, and perhaps clouds with interesting shapes? Take it in. What do you see? If you've worked deep into the nighttime, do you see stars, or the moon? Whatever it is, I guarantee it will rise higher than the ceiling of your vestibule – and height offers perspective.

Give yourself a break and allow yourself to make the most of that 75 percent of time spent away from the job. If you find yourself consumed in your career, ask yourself whether you truly love spending so many hours in that endeavor or whether you are simply hesitant to change because that is all you know. If you do love your work and career, you are blessed. If this is true, do you sing the praises of your job and share that positive energy with those around you?

How do you speak about your job to others? Do you complain? Have you been complaining for weeks, months, years? If so, ask yourself why you would do something for so long and just complain about it. If it is hot in your house on a summer day, do you sit there and complain or get up and turn on a fan?

If you find yourself constantly complaining, it's high time to make a change. You can control your destiny. If you complain regularly to simply get sympathy from others, that time would be better spent figuring out your next step so you can begin to focus on what truly could make you happy. If you feel like complaining, do so while looking in the mirror. The solution will be staring you in the face.

That doesn't mean you should march up to the boss and quit today. We all have responsibilities and realities in life, such as rent, mortgage payments, credit card bills, a family to support, and so much more. *The Break Equation* is not an exercise to encourage impulsive irresponsibility. Rather, it encourages acting on responsible ambition.

Only you can define where that line falls in your life and no one else. But once you recognize where your dreams lie and whether your job is in line with them, you have a perspective that will help you know what to do next and when. If you feel thwarted, as if you have hit that ceiling, consider it a positive break that you recognize how you are being held back. You will be ready to act.

And you can start small. If you want to write a cookbook, write down that first recipe. If you want to write a movie script, write down a few scenes or sketch out your plot. If you want to work in an animal shelter, volunteer one weekend a month. If you want to open a catering company, find someone who can help you put up a simple web page, buy a few business cards, and hand them out and see what happens. Just getting started will fuel your passion. If you don't act even in a small way, then your talk has simply been empty. Perhaps you really don't have that passion after all if you are not motivated even to get started in those small ways. You need some wood in the stove before the fire can actually burn.

If you feel your job is blocking your dreams, remember that your job can only block you for a portion of your available time each day. The rest is up to you. Nor should you count yourself short by thinking of your eight nightly hours of sleep as time wasted. Yes, most of us spend as much time sleeping as we do on the job, but the time spent in slumber and dreams is far from inconsequential.

In expanding your horizons, your time under the covers is as important as your waking hours away from work. There is no glass ceiling when you dream.

Of course we all have things that weigh on our minds, nights when we wake up worried about work or tasks that we need to accomplish. Did you write that check to the bank? Did you send that crucial e-mail to a customer? Your daily agenda invades your night, ready to take over again as soon as the alarm clock beckons you back to the rat race. Our minds are ever busy trying to resolve our issues, small and large.

Amid that swirl of concerns, your subconscious wants to know this: Are you truly happy? A night's sleep may reenergize your body, but what does it do for your soul? In our sleep we do have visions of happiness at times. We feel joy. We draw near to our loved ones. We picture ourselves in new careers, pursuing new adventures. This is prime time for growth and rejuvenation of body and mind. Sleep offers us a fresh start – not just to a new day, but to new opportunities.

When I sleep, my mind often wanders freely – not just to my daily tasks but also, at times, to visions of new ideas, exotic places to visit, extraordinary people to meet, adventures to experience, products to build. I love to dream, and am often surprised by the creativity that arrives at night.

In my life I have embarked on a variety of entrepreneurial endeavors, and it's during sleep that those ideas often gel. I envision a new creation, a chapter of a book, or a trip I could take. The concepts are not always grand, but they are certainly concrete. I conceive of a conversation I need to have with a loved one. I picture myself with friends as yet unknown to me. The perceptions sometimes flow so fast and free that I risk losing them forever when I awake to daily cares.

Elias Howe, inventor of the sewing machine, told of a dream he had after falling asleep deeply frustrated. He had been unable to develop a needle that would make mechanical sewing possible. In his dream, he said, savages thrust spears back and forth at him – and near the tip of each spear was a hole. Problem solved. What a loss if he had let that dream slip away.

Like those of you who have traveled for work, I'm often a bit lonely on the road, yet I find that the excitement of new cities sparks more vivid dreams. Sometimes those dreams contain intriguing ideas, and I need to write them down on the spot – but it can be hard enough to find a specific street while traveling, let alone a pad and pen.

That's why I've made it a priority to keep stationery ready by the bedside to immediately record those post-midnight musings from which I awake. That way I can remember them, come sunrise. I often turn to my collection of nightstand notes for inspiration.

On our website (www.TheBreakEquation.com), you can download the Nightstand Notes as pictured here. Print out several and keep them by your bedside, just in case. Or better yet, design your own notes, with a theme or colors that encourage you. Just don't use your company stationery if you hate your job.

After you jot down those dreams, promise yourself to try to catch them. Do more than talk about what you might do someday. Tomorrow, when that alarm clock rings, let it stir not just your body to action but also your soul. Pursue at least one of your dreams into the daylight hours.

It's so easy to see the stars and moon at night – they shine so brightly that you feel you could touch them – and though you lose sight of them as you go about your daily tasks, you can be assured of this: The stars and the moon are still there. You can still reach for them. No glass ceiling can stop you.

+ − × ÷

Are you an optimistic or pessimistic person? What people and events, both good and bad, have shaped your soul and the way that you think as of this moment?

I often wonder how I came to think the way I do today regarding my career and business passions. I am a risk taker, continually searching for new endeavors and challenges – whether a friendly wager on a golf game or a trip to an exotic land.

Likewise, I admire entrepreneurs and people who take calculated business risks, to whatever extreme fits their risk profile, in the pursuit of wealth and self-fulfillment. There are certainly many factors other than money that can define a "rich" or "wealthy" life – such as health, family, friends, travel, and more. However, in any business, money does matter. It cannot buy happiness, but it helps. I read recently that one's quality of life doesn't change much once earnings exceed $75,000, yet I believe money can buy access to opportunity – and the opportunity to pay it forward, a concept that we will discuss later.

As for me, I yearn for the big win, the 300-yard drive in golf, the sale of a company with a multimillion-dollar payoff, or the invention that everyone must have. I respect people with novel ideas who act on them, win or lose, embracing failure as a step toward success.

In truth, failure and success are not that far apart. In golf, the difference between a 68.5 scoring average and a 69.7 may be the difference between global success and obscurity as a professional golfer. You may be only one or two putts away from being the next Fred Couples, yet the reality is that you are barely getting by on the PGA Tour, struggling to make your financial ends meet. However, that doesn't mean you're a failure at golf.

Which is worse: Failure, or failure to act? I admire those who have failed, kept trying, and risen to even greater heights. Sure, the heartache of a failed attempt can linger, but what matters is how quickly you bounce back. Failure at one time or another is simply part of an ambitious life and we need to view those events as part of the journey rather than a destination. Every day is another opportunity to make a positive change to get ourselves back on track towards fulfilling our dreams – and we can make great progress by taking small steps, day by day. Continue to push yourself, to set new ambitious goals, and encourage others to do the same.

My father, Mike, played baseball in high school. In 1964, in his senior year at St. Benedict's Prep in New Jersey, he came to the plate in the Greater Newark Tournament championship game. With two strikes against him and his team down 2-1, he hit a game-winning single to right field.

In my life, I have heard my father say many times that you can get into the Baseball Hall of Fame in two ways. One way is to get up to bat every time and swing for the stars. If you are good (and with a little luck), you will hit a lot of home runs. But often you will strike out. The other way is to hit a lot of singles, with more control and consistency in how you approach the game.

My father's strategy has led to his success not only in baseball but also in life. I admire him for his tremendous work ethic, something that he inherited from his dad who was a mechanic who owned a Gulf Oil gas station and operated it from 6 a.m. to 6 p.m., six days a week, for sixty years. The sacrifices that these men made for their families have been one of the foundational, positive breaks I have had in my life.

Perhaps my father's winning ways were accelerated with that 1964 single that drove in the game-winning run. His teammates carried him off the field that day on their shoulders – and my father has long carried his family on his shoulders. Certainly that single was a break for his team. In reflection, it was break for our family, too, establishing his steady, consistent, and successful approach to life.

Cal Ripken was one of my sports idols when I was a child. He is perhaps best known for breaking New York Yankees first baseman Lou Gehrig's record for consecutive games played of 2,130, a record many deemed unbreakable. He surpassed the 56-year-old record in 1995 and went on to set a new consecutive game record of 2,632 games by the time he retired from his 21-year career with the Baltimore Orioles

Although Cal did hit 431 home runs over the span of his career, it is his perseverance and consistency that he is most often remembered for. In contrast, Reggie Jackson, another childhood hero, is known for both his 563 career home runs and his Major League Baseball record of 2,597 career strikeouts. Different style players, different statistics – yet they both share a home today in the Baseball Hall of Fame.

Often, when people look at the big swingers, they see how often they strike out. In business, only you can determine which pitches you will swing at, and when, as we all have different risk profiles at different times in life. In my business life, I have a risk profile that drives me to swing for the fences at times. To date, my batting average is respectable but certainly not worthy of the all-star roster. Yet the lower on-base percentage that comes with a few extra strikeouts doesn't concern me. I am looking for the right pitch, and until I find it, I'm prepared to be called out swinging.

None of us is strictly a home run hitter, nor does anyone hit solely singles. We are not that one-dimensional. We have vast opportunities and skills, and the way we swing at the ball should depend upon the pitch delivered and what's happening on the field. While my dad's moment on the field came in 1964 due to a single, he has certainly hit a few home runs in life as well. And while I continue to swing for the fences, I still manage to get on base from time to time.

However, we all need to reflect and evaluate our strategies. Calculating your Break Score is one of those opportunities. Do you secretly wish you could change your swing? Have you become too comfortable in your routine, your career, and your income? Perhaps it's time to change bats or talk to a swing coach.

Your success and your struggles don't necessarily mean your approach has been right or wrong. I love the diversity in life and the fact that people can "make it" in more ways than one. A home run slugger shouldn't tell the batter who hits singles that he'll only reach the Hall of Fame by swinging harder. Likewise, the guy with the high on-base percentage shouldn't tell the home run hitter to stop striking out.

We all need to spend less time and effort trying to change other people's lives and simply appreciate and learn from their approach. No one person has it right, but we all have the ability to make it right in our own lives. How hard you swing when you're at the plate isn't what matters. What's important is that you have the confidence to step up to the plate.

I've yet to hit the big home run in life. Yes, I have hit the long ball. Some have even bounced over the fence for a ground rule double. And often, when I fall asleep at night, I think of my strategy for the next time I'm at bat. I ponder what I can do differently, what skills I can call on to help give myself a break.

I wish I had the answer or the "secret sauce" to make magic happen tomorrow. But I'm still searching, just like many of you. I'm confident in my approach and passionate about what I'm trying to do in life. I'm trying to put my philosophies into action, to follow my ambitions, to live the fulfilled life. Life is short, whether we live till 25 or 95, and we must dare to be ourselves. We all have value and have so much to contribute, and now is the time to get back on track.

In the years ahead, if I hit a few grand slams, it will certainly be rewarding. But what's most fulfilling is the journey, believing anything is possible and putting my words into action. Win or lose, it is the pursuit that I find intriguing. If you feel ambitions stirring, give yourself a break and take this call to action. That's what turns dreams into realities.

When I was a child, I never thought that my grandfather let me win at checkers. And when I won, I felt as much like a king as the many checker pieces I capped on the board. I thought I was making all the right moves. I realize now that my grandfather was really the one making the good move: He nurtured in me a confidence and a winning spirit that serves me well today. Knowing him was a major break in my life. I'll tell you more about this remarkable man later in the book.

By knowing more about yourself, you can recognize the breaks that come your way and seize opportunities rather than squander them. *The Break Equation* is one tool to help you do that.

So often, the decisions we make seem no more significant than flipping a coin. We leave our dreams to chance. Heads, we accept a new job, tails we tough it out another year. Heads, we move to a new city, tails we don't. That's about as much thought as we give to even profound matters, since we find it hard to predict how the game will play out.

And when you do come to a decision, others may try to dissuade you, and you might find it hard to tune them out. The naysayers will tell you your dream is impossible. Let them have their opinions. Just remember this: It only takes an opinion to judge someone, but it takes courage to act.

If you aren't taking action, ask yourself why. Is it because you will be going against the opinion of someone you respect? Consider whether that person might be discouraging you to meet his or her own agenda. Be confident of the value of your ambitions: Even if you don't succeed in your pursuit, you will gain experience by learning what it takes to launch something different, whether an idea, a company, or a cause. Those who have never stood in your shoes, the naysayers, have only their opinion to offer – and it is important to keep that influence in perspective.

If you are seeking motivation around one of your business ideas, make it a priority to surround yourself with people who have a similar passion and a similar ambition. They will understand – and they'll have the perspective and encouragement you need to drive you towards success. And when you do hit that home run or game-winning single, you will be ever closer to realizing that anything is possible - somewhere far beyond that glass ceiling.

CHAPTER 3:

RED WINE WISHES

We had just opened our third bottle, a very special Silver Oak 1996 from Napa Valley. The wine had been flowing, as had the conversation and laughter, when the subject turned to, well, wine.

I tapped the table: "How about this!" I said. "What if we all moved to Massachusetts and ran a wine store or two together?"

My wife, Annabelle, and I, newlyweds at the time just back from our honeymoon, were out with our good friends Mike and Kelly for dinner one night in Washington, D.C. We all often enjoyed talking of our daydreams together, about the endless possibilities in life. Where would we all be in one, five, or ten years? What would our careers look like in fifteen or twenty? What could we do differently to make more money and enjoy life more? What kind of wine would we be drinking when we all had dinner someday when we met up in Miami, London, or Sydney?

"Not just a wine store or two, how about we buy a vineyard, you know? Or invest in one, and go up there and run it," Mike said. "Why not?"

We all looked at one another, considering the possibility and envisioning the lifestyle, focusing on the positives despite the challenges of running such a business.

"My aunt and uncle – they're up there," Mike said, "and they're already in the wine business. We could learn a lot from them."

"I can see us now," said Annabelle. "We have this country house, and the four of us are out on the back patio, and we invite our friends and families up all of the time."

"That's right," said Kelly. "And we'd bring out our best bottles, and pull the cork on the very best year."

"A very good year, every year, forever," I said. "Why don't we go up there and check out some land and see where it goes – maybe we could all be partners, you know – in a vineyard."

Now, none of us knew anything about running a vineyard. And we all had jobs waiting for us in the morning. None of us was prepared to pick up stakes and move to Massachusetts.

But we could – if we set our minds to it. If we could imagine it, we could do it. And our imaginings, like wine, morphed and changed with every new toast. There we were, great friends in our mid-30s, hard-working and dreaming hard.

I smiled at Annabelle, and then glanced at Mike, who was swirling the Silver Oak in his glass. I knew his mind was working through the logistics.

We were full of red wine wishes that night, and as quickly as one dream formed, the next one surfaced: "What if we ran a golf resort down in Southern California?"

It was time to order another bottle – or two.

+   −   ×   ÷

I dreamed that night of grapes hanging heavy on the vine. I dreamed of a villa in Italy where we'd talked so many times of living and working, basking in the culture. I dreamed of a hilly Southern fairway, a grassy expanse to the ocean.

My dreams were a parade of all the fantasies we'd shared over wine on so many such nights but had yet to fulfill, once we woke up and returned to the reality of our lives. This was a good life, yes, but what of our passions? Never mind those "champagne wishes and caviar dreams" that Robin Leach embraced on *Lifestyles of the Rich and Famous* – what would become of our own red wine wishes?

When I awoke that Saturday morning, I poured some coffee and sat on the couch, thinking about the dinner conversation. I reached for my running shoes. Today, I resolved, I would act. I would go for a run, and before I returned I would know just what I would do. I would take a definitive first step toward a dream.

I would give myself a break.

Unlike most times when I went on a run, I didn't turn on my iPod that morning. I wanted to think. I set rules for this run: I would think only forward, not back, resisting thoughts of prior mistakes. I would daydream and think only positively. And whether I would run two minutes or two hours, I resolved to come home with a new idea. I was looking for a break, and I was setting out on this Saturday to find one.

By the time I returned, I had conceived of *The Break Equation* and had sketched out in my mind a chapter or two of a book I would write – the book you are holding. The only thing that remained was my commitment to act on my idea – to overcome the self-doubt of whether I could actually write a book. Who am I to be an author? I knew that I was not the only guy who thought he had a good book idea. After all, I imagine you probably have one as well. However, I also knew that only action would turn my musings into print.

What had gelled for me was the truth that each of us is the product of all that has happened to us, good or bad. Our experiences add or subtract from our joys and ambitions. They can be divisive, or exponentially positive. Such is the human equation, and each of us reacts uniquely to these experiences. We are shaped by the equation, but it doesn't define us: In short, life is what we make of it.

As we all get older, life's complications continue to set in. There are endless reasons to say that today is not quite the right time to do something, but perhaps tomorrow will be right. Yes, our daily responsibilities often prevail, but we must not forget that our passions are a responsibility, too. Life's busyness shouldn't get in the way of our heart's desires. One must commit oneself to try.

We are all not that different from one another. Our neighbors on different streets or different continents most likely have dreams that are not unlike our own. And I'm certain that many of them also defer those dreams as they attend to life's responsibilities and postpone them day to day until, eventually, the fire goes out.

Life sweeps all of us along from birth to bills and beyond, and we find increasingly less time for our dreams. Soon, they only seem to resurface over a bottle of wine, or at 3 a.m. as we gaze at the ceiling, wondering about the stars.

As I ran, I thought long and hard about my successes and failures - and about the breaks I already had in life. I tried to think about them in a different way, reflecting on how I had reacted to those bad breaks, considering if my reaction to them may actually be impacting my confidence or holding me back in some way. Likewise, I thought about how those good breaks can serve even more as a source of motivation. What I resolved to do as I ran that morning was to develop a new tool, a new way of thinking about a break in life, to help people reignite the spark – and to step forward in living the dream that they desire.

As I mentioned earlier, I went to college at Villanova University near Philadelphia, Pennsylvania. Upon graduation, I wasn't sure what I wanted to do, but I interviewed with GE Healthcare (then GE Medical Systems) for a corporate training program resulting in a sales account management role. I joined a great company with quality people and training, a great opportunity for anyone, especially a rookie. I took it all in, and worked hard. I had the opportunity to live in various places in the US and travel extensively. For a kid who grew up in a suburban New Jersey town, living 3,000 miles away from home on my own was a daunting task. Yet I knew deep-down it was an opportunity worth taking and one that I was ready for, even though I was outside my comfort zone in many ways at the beginning.

My first real responsibility was to sell radiology equipment, which I ended up doing pretty well. I'll never forget the day in my fourth year with the company when I secured a contract for medical equipment to be installed throughout a brand new hospital in Maryland. It culminated over fifteen months of hard work delivered by a broad team of people who worked tirelessly towards this goal. My commission for that one deal was close to six-figures, all in one check – something I could not previously have imagined.

That night, I went out for dinner with a college buddy, Doug, and we ordered $55 steaks and $35 single-malt scotches in the lobby of the Four Seasons Hotel in Washington. I was in my mid-twenties and, for the moment, felt rich and proud. We talked that night of our single-malt wishes rather than red wine ones. It was a rewarding feeling, and the success fueled my ambition for more.

I was driven to meet as many people as possible and my GE networking led me to a gentlemen named Joe, a retired Colonel in the US Air Force and the Director of Federal Programs for GE Medical Systems. Due to internal reorganization, he needed someone to sell to and manage the US military hospital accounts in Western Europe. After a rigorous test trip (as I call it) to Germany to see how I would perform, he extended the opportunity to me to manage all of Western Europe. This global opportunity at such a young age was – and remains – a multiplying break in my life, one that only drove my hunger for travel and global opportunity further.

In those early career days, I was learning the culture of sales, a meritocracy in which success is based on results. I found it to be extraordinarily entrepreneurial. However, there was no security blanket. If I didn't successfully sell our products, I didn't get paid. While the carrot of the six-figure payday was the goal, there were certainly many zero-dollar days in between. I started to consider the alternative, such as a salaried position, where that uncertainty could be eliminated.

During the darker zero-dollar paydays, I would often question what value my position had in society – what was I contributing? Was that really what my value in life was? You may have had similar moments. Putting it all in perspective, those dark days were a call to action, to either get out there and knock on more doors to find that golden sale or to find a new job, a new opportunity.

For me, the big sales commission was exciting and motivational. My paycheck was based not on the number of days I showed up at work but on the results of the time devoted. Success came down to this: If ten doors were closed in my face, could I handle the eleventh? After all, behind it might just be that next $55 steak and $35 single-malt scotch waiting.

+   −   ×   ÷

In the workforce, the pay scale can become how we measure our value. If you have a $40,000 job, you may come to feel that that is your worth in life. That financial glass ceiling may be a barrier to your self-worth, your self-confidence, though there may be little real difference between the person who earns $40,000 and the person who earns $400,000 – or $4 million. One certainly has more money but does not have more value in life.

We all have responsibilities and need stability, particularly when young and with fewer resources. We may stick with a job that allows us to make our way in life. We may not see that the job has become a glass ceiling to our earlier ambitions. That realization itself can be a critical break in life – the recognition that you yearn for more.

At this moment, you have identified that you are in what I call your Just-in-Case-Career, or JICC. If you realize you are in a JICC, that doesn't mean you don't work hard or long enough. A JICC is not in itself a bad thing, unless it goes unrecognized.

How do you recognize a JICC? Consider whether you love what you do. Consider how much you complain about it.

If you do love what you do, then embrace it and cherish it, for surely you wake up every day with a sense of passion and fulfillment. Share your story with others and help them identify how you were able to reach that peaceful place in life.

But if you don't love your job, then acknowledge that and make up your mind to keep seeking a new path. Once you recognize that you are in a JICC, you have made a very important evaluation of your life. You are preparing to follow your dream.

Perhaps that JICC will always be in your life, as a sense of income and stability, as you work on your passions. The victory comes in acknowledging how you really feel and finding ways to follow your vision, the mission for your life. Remember, a job is not a career. It is only one step in the journey of your dreams.

If monotony sets in and you find yourself complaining about the glass ceiling, look in the mirror: The nature of your job may not be likely to change, but you certainly can. Are you willing to bet on yourself and do what is required? If you want something more, you have to seek it out.

Even with my success at GE, I had that burning ambition for something of my own. When I told others about my ideas, they sometimes would laugh. They would call them impossible or unrealistic. "Don't quit your day job," they would say, or they would offer a dismissive "good luck with that." It bothered me. Why did they think so little of me or of my ability to accomplish more? What was so great about my day job, or theirs? Did they lack confidence in me – or in their own ability to accomplish such "unrealistic" goals?

I enjoyed my time at GE and respected those I met along the way, but I could not deny some empty feeling in my heart. I felt I had more to contribute, more to risk. I felt an untapped potential. I wanted to feel that I was stretching outside my comfort zone. That feeling I'd had when I made my first sales call at GE had disappeared. I was eager to find it again.

When I was a senior member of my golf team at Don Bosco High School in Ramsey, New Jersey, there came a day when I had to tee-off for the first time in front of a gallery of people. I'd hit a drive off the first tee hundreds of times, but this time so many people were watching. A photographer from the local paper was snapping pictures. I can't even remember how I did. I was that nervous.

But when you have that feeling in the pit of your stomach, you can be certain of one thing: You are growing. Maybe that uncomfortable shot will soar, or maybe you'll cut an ugly divot. Regardless of the result, that shot has added tremendous value in your life to assist with what you do next. You're sure to feel just a bit less nervous the next time that situation surfaces, because you're becoming used to the new atmosphere. You know what you expect of yourself.

My attitude from then on was this: "Snap those pictures, examine my swing, it doesn't matter." I didn't let the pressure stop me from trying. Once you get in a few good shots, your confidence grows – and confidence builds on itself. It has a multiplying effect. Some people fear public speaking, for example, but through small steps they could conquer that fear. They could talk to a school class, or say a few words to their congregation – and by feeling good about overcoming the nervousness and doing just fine, they'd be motivated to try bigger audiences.

I was eager for that feeling in my stomach once again. I was ready to expand, to conquer new challenges. I wasn't trying to get out of what I was doing at that time – it was that I was excited and ready to step into my ambitions. A lot of people, frustrated with their jobs, say, "I want to get out!" But are they really trying to get out? Or are they trying to get into what they really want to do? Thinking about it that way would give them the positive perspective that might just be the catalyst for change.

I have often maintained and managed my own JICC, but I can't understand those who complain about the fundamental nature of what they do, yet won't look further. To so many people, a job is good or bad based on the hours, benefits package, weeks of vacation, or variety of food in the cafeteria. Why settle for a job that, yes, pays the bills but leaves one yearning for fulfillment, yearning to do something different?

Dreaming, after all, can be motivating and beautiful. What sort of dreams do we wish for our children? Do we hope they go to sleep just to be tormented by visions of strife and violence? Do we tell them bedtime stories of crime and poverty? Or do we wish them Disney dreams with images of far-away lands?

A friend of mine, John, likes to say I have a Disney World approach to life. I tend to see the positive nature in people and events. I am passionate about people, life, and ideas. It's not that I think the world is a magical kingdom, but I do value one's capacity to imagine.

I like to focus on why things can be done rather than why they can't. I subscribe to the words of George Bernard Shaw, as famously paraphrased by Robert F. Kennedy: "*There are those who look at things the way they are and ask why. I dream of things that never were and ask why not?*"

I often read Disney stories to my nieces at bedtime. When they fall fast asleep, I like to think they are vividly imagining Mickey Mouse and friends singing and dancing. The realities of life come soon enough for all of us in life. In childhood, we need to hold on to our imagination. I have come to embrace being called "Disney World" because it conjures a life fueled by imagination. Anything seems possible. That's not a bad thing to want for our children. That's not a bad thing to want for ourselves at times.

After all, Disney World is a happy place to visit, where the Disney team hopes to leave people feeling optimistic about the world and dreaming about all that is possible. Yet, so many people leave the theme park or the Disney movie and quickly lose that positive glow – or even revert to negativity, focusing on why a dream of their own can't happen or diminishing those of others. I find that people tend to focus on what they think other people may be doing wrong rather than focusing on what they should change in their own lives.

Those who try to dim your dreams are perhaps jealous of your open spirit – the one they may have lost long ago. They attribute others' success to luck, or perhaps cheating, rather than effort. Lacking confidence in the ability to make their own dreams a reality, they may elevate themselves by trying to bring others down. When you hear such comments, offer a firm handshake, thank them for their thoughts – and walk away to look up at the stars. Be thankful that you can see beyond the ceiling.

+   −   ×   ÷

The naysayers couldn't get to me. I wasn't afraid to fail. I'd heard so many accounts of people of all ages who were following their dreams. Whether they succeeded or fell short (as many did) wasn't the point. What I admired is that they had ambitious dreams and they stepped up to the plate to try.

I looked in the mirror and asked myself if I would take a shot or sit around complaining about what others were doing, being envious of the opportunity they had created for themselves. I realized that my inhibitions had nothing to do with skills or talents that others had and I was lacking – it only had to do with confidence. Never believe someone else can accomplish something that you cannot. If they can do it, so can I. And so can you. This was my call to action.

I investigated some options and decided to purchase an advertising board system. The system was basically a lighted panel with space for dozens of advertisements. The owner would install it in a hotel lobby and sell that advertising space to local businesses. Guests would come to the lobby and use a phone connected to the board to call toll free for take-out, movie tickets, or a taxi. The board was certainly not an e-commerce solution as we may think of one today, but at the time I hoped to make a dent in the Washington tourism and advertising market.

I recruited a small team to help bring the vision to reality, wrote a business plan, and pursued the idea for hours, night after night. We successfully installed the system in our first location and even sold a few ads. We spent over 18 months of sweat equity on this endeavor, attempting to raise funding to expand with a more modern kiosk model in malls and airports around the country. While we all had our JICCs, we found as many hours per week as possible to drive the business forward.

So many people have ideas, but so few actually try them. Up until this point, that had described me. Now, by stepping forward, I was able to grow. I gained a deep respect for the multitude of challenges associated with running a start-up. In the past, I might have called success stories a matter of luck. Now, I understood the intensity of the process and the risk associated with such a venture. Win or lose, entrepreneurs assume the risk. They are less focused on their on-base percentage. Instead, they focus on looking for the right pitch without fear of the strikeout holding them back.

Opening one new business doesn't make a person an entrepreneur. One is an action (certainly an entrepreneurial one) but the other is a mindset that will separate the two by the way they not only see opportunity but also assume the risk to act. Neither is right or wrong. One is not more prone to success than the other. But one certainly carries a higher degree of risk.

Shortly after we launched the advertising company in 2001, our country faced the September 11th terrorist attacks, and travel slowed dramatically, especially in the nation's capital. It was not a good time for us to be asking small businesses and hotels to spend money. Should we call off our endeavor, or change our strategy? I decided that we could help the travel industry rebound and drive new business to small, local enterprises. I had learned a lesson in the entrepreneurial life: Be prepared to change your strategy to adapt to new realities.

We persevered a few more months. In the end, however, we were not able to secure the private funding that we needed to implement the kiosk system and had to shut down. Through this failed opportunity, what had we accomplished? We had taken one advertising board and expanded that into a creative national model, in which multiple larger companies expressed interest. We had developed a network of entrepreneurial people to whom I was certain I would be reaching out to in the future, and they to me. We had learned some valuable lessons. I was surprised to learn that although I was disappointed, I did not feel defeated – just more ambitious and eager to find that next opportunity, and soon.

One of the advertising boards ended up in my home storage unit, where it still sits today. One day I will install it in the basement of my house for my kids to call for a pizza, movie tickets, or flowers. I'm not sure how it will be used in function, but it will always serve in spirit as a reminder to me of the importance of acting on a dream. As it sits idle, I will try not to think of the sunk cost associated with the venture in any other way than as an investment in my passions.

What makes a venture worthwhile? It's not all about money or fame. It's about following your dreams. It's about the pursuit of a personal mission that fuels your passions, both in life and in business.

Again, never mind the naysayers. Most likely, they have never tried to do what you are attempting to do, and they have certainly not been walking in your shoes. Only you can define whether a venture is worthwhile, and it will not be a failure if you decline to perceive it as one. Instead, take away the valuable lessons, step back and evaluate what you will do differently next time.

Hanging up my spikes was never an option. I couldn't imagine that. I had just overcome a tough personal barrier by deciding to act, and I felt more energized than ever for my next attempt. Ideas were flowing freely.

At this time in my life, I had the opportunity to take a few JICC-related road trips with a buddy named Chris. As kids, we were highly competitive. We would set up a tennis court in the driveway, making the net out of trash cans and marking the lines with tape. On a sunny July afternoon in New Jersey, we would be battling in the finals at the U.S. Open. If it wasn't tennis, we would be shootings hoops, or playing ping-pong in the basement. We both had the same goal in mind – to win. And as we got older, that spirit translated into an entrepreneurial drive, and at times we have joined forces. That's what we did during those road trips.

Chris is four years younger than me, and after several years spent in corporate America he was starting to question what he was meant to do in his career. We had many hours to talk and daydream on those trips, and we came up with some great ideas. I must admit, we came up with our share of bad ideas as well – yet even the worst ideas can help to stimulate the next thought, the next invention, and the next break.

We decided that we would work hard and try to turn our ideas into reality. We bought two marble notebooks to chronicle our ideas, our plans, and our time frames. The goal was five years out; by that time, we intended to make our entrance into Hollywood.

At that time, reality TV was taking off, so many of the ideas that we developed were focused on that niche. I'll share a few of them here, and you can decide for yourself whether they fall into the good or bad bucket!

After watching a revolutionary first year of *American Idol,* we wrote a reality TV treatment that we called *LA Dream,* focusing on a dance competition with elimination in a similar format. We also wrote a screenplay called *8 College Nights,* following a week in the life of six college seniors.

After extensive networking, we had the break of being offered a meeting with a Hollywood producer to talk about *8 College Nights*. I flew to Los Angeles to pitch it to him in Beverly Hills at a Starbucks on Wilshire Boulevard. I could see the Hollywood sign in the mountains behind me. I was so ready for this break.

I will never forget the anticipation. I woke up early that day, went for a run to get my mind in order, had a good lunch, and showed up, screenplay in hand, fifteen minutes early. The producer was fifteen minutes late. After coffee and a brief read, he said he would be back in touch. A few weeks passed when he finally called to say he liked the concept but that he felt it was too generic.

Chris and I rewrote the script around fraternity/sorority life in college. We called him shortly thereafter with a revised version, called *College Greeks,* which didn't seem to change his opinion too much. So we kept writing.

Cabin Fever was next, and one of the best, in our opinion. Imagine this: A cruise ship takes business executives out to sea with a handful of contestants trying to compete for their attention as they present their business ideas. It was one of the first business-related spins on the blossoming reality TV market. Again, through shameless networking, we had the opportunity to pitch the head of reality TV at CBS. He was a gracious person with his time and encouragement, but he said "the time wasn't right" at his network for such a show.

We kept writing. We created a TV anchor reality show called *The Future of Today* to find the next Katie Couric and Matt Lauer. We continued to network and to knock on doors, most of which closed right in our face. The effort was frustrating, but we maintained our passions nonetheless. Even today, while our portfolio remains on the shelf awaiting the right opportunity, we know we were taking shots and following our ambitions.

My wife, Annabelle, is an interior designer and avid equestrian – so not long after we met, I approached her with a TV show idea called *Pet Designers*.

"Take *Extreme Makeover: Home Edition*," I explained, "and combine it with the fascination that people have with their pets. Our designers would pick one lucky furry friend each episode and build its master a custom home design. If you're a Yankees fan, maybe we'd build a Yankee Stadium dog house."

At the beginning of our relationship, Annabelle may have questioned my sanity from time to time, but she has come to understand and share some of these passions and ambitions. Together, we found a way to present the script to producers at the Discovery channel and, sadly, they passed.

However, it was a great opportunity to explore, and one that sparked a new entrepreneurial part of our life together. Today, she is pursuing her own passion with an interior design business (www.StylishFurnitureAndDecor.com). And, one day when we have a yard, there just may be that custom doghouse replica of Yankee Stadium waiting for the dog.

Outside of the Hollywood ambitions, I continued to look for unique products or needs, an opening perhaps for the next must-have gadget, game, or gimmick. One spring, at a Dave Matthews concert in Charlottesville, Virginia, I was tailgating before the show with my friends and, as at any good tailgate, we were having a few drinks, laughing, and tossing a football around. However, there was too much traffic to have much of a football game, so we ended up spending most of our time right around our car.

We made up a game of trying to throw tennis balls into the trunk of our car from farther and farther away; the farther back we went, the more points we could score. An idea was born: Why not design a car-trunk game system specifically marketed for the tailgating world? Once again, that next morning, I felt called to action. I recently had read Tim Ferris' *4-Hour Work Week* and felt motivated by his advice and resources. Acting on the idea, I decided to hire a graphic designer to help put my vision on paper. Within a few weeks, we had a graphical representation, a logo, and some marketing material.

I committed to do whatever it would take to push the concept forward. I manufactured several prototypes in China, attended trade shows, and, after examining the market, decided to expand on the tailgate system to brand it also as a children's play system. Parents could buy our collapsible game frame system and simply swap game covers when the kids would bore of a particular game. They could save money – and space. I was confident that this concept had potential in the licensing world. It won't come as a surprise to you that I could easily envision a line of Disney character inspired game covers – and so much more.

After months of phone calls and sending samples and marketing material around the world, I gained the attention of a major toy licensing agent. I pursued any and every angle to develop and license the product. Whatever it took, I wanted to get it onto store shelves.

I acted on an idea. I channeled the skills from previous endeavors, successful or not, into an exciting new one. In my mind, that was success. No matter how the product would eventually do on the market, I knew I'd just had one of my more significant breaks in life.

+   –   ×   ÷

"Genius is one percent inspiration, and ninety-nine percent perspiration," Thomas Edison said. I had certainly put my share of sweat-equity hours into my endeavors, rising early and working late into the evenings to pursue these ambitions while still attending to my JICC and life's responsibilities.

It is said that Edison failed a thousand times while trying to invent the light bulb. When asked about it, the story goes, he responded: "I have not failed one thousand times. I have successfully discovered one thousand ways to *not* make a light bulb."

I wonder how he felt after those 999 discoveries. "Many of life's failures," he is quoted as saying, "are people who did not realize how close they were to success when they gave up."

Likewise, as Babe Ruth once said, "Every strike brings me closer to the next home run." We must remember that.

I believe we need to build a culture where failure is encouraged. How can creativity and innovation thrive when failure is punished? "Failures are a gift," wrote A.G. Lafley, former chief executive officer of Procter & Gamble. "Unless you view them that way, you won't learn from failure."

I'll never lose the desire to create for myself, to attempt to build businesses, to make something from nothing. I'm not sure what gene I have that drives me in this way, but I have it for better or worse and I have learned to embrace it.

I appreciate the jobs and opportunities that I have had so far in life. They have given me the compensation, confidence and the wisdom to go out there and try to pursue my passions. They have introduced me to a tremendous network of people. They help me to keep my passions alive – and those passions are what drive me. I try to live an optimistic life, where I pursue my dreams as often as possible. My approach is not the right way, or the wrong. It is simply my journey. I don't want to be asking myself in ten years why I didn't try.

Do you recall my philosophy that no one job defines your career? It's also true that no one venture defines your success in the journey of your entrepreneurial mission. We never know what may be around that next corner, and only you can determine what is worthwhile on your journey.

My hope is that *The Break Equation* encourages you to think deeply and personally about your life, what it means, what has happened, and where you want to take it. Are you holding back your dreams because of stereotypes about what your obligations should be? Are you holding yourself back because of a lack of confidence over a past failure? Are you trying to find that passion you once had? Are you asking and looking for a break in life?

This book is not a comprehensive guide on how to launch an idea or a company, or how to develop a product and take it to market. Instead, it offers you a new tool to help you evaluate the events and people in your life, to put them in perspective, perhaps in a different light, to see a past event in a new way that may free you from a prior inhibition. It will help you to understand those unique factors that motivate you which may lead you to a delightful course of action with your next business idea and ambition.

The chapters that follow will examine breaks in life from various angles, including good breaks that end up with a negative result, bad breaks that end up with a positive result, and breaks that just never seem to happen. Good fortune is wonderful – but must we wait for it? We all have the power to make change happen today. What we need is a renewed belief in ourselves. We need confidence.

The Break Equation is the latest chapter in the story of my entrepreneurial life, my quest for fulfillment and success. I hope it leads you to yours.

Success can come as a full-time or part-time job. It can come in pursuit of a lifelong passion, or one that comes to you tonight over that glass of wine. You can go after your dream publicly or privately. You may have little to invest, or millions of dollars.

You need not be on the cover of *Forbes* to be a great success. No one has to pat you on the back or say "job well done." Those things are nice but not the goal. You are a success when you wake up every day with a sense of fulfillment – and no regrets.

Success is never forgetting those red wine wishes.

Chapter 4:

FORMULA FOR FULFILLMENT

As a child, I loved playing ping-pong with my father. As we played long, heated matches in our basement, one of us would inevitably make a shot that would hit the net, linger there for a moment, and then drop to one side or the other. Sometimes it fell in my favor, sometimes it did not.

At that moment, no matter which side the ball fell, my father would call out, "It bent, but it wouldn't break!" At the time, I was either elated by victory or pained by defeat. I think back now to those matches and the deeper meaning in life. Are there really good and bad breaks that determine life's course, or is it how we react to those events that really matters?

Most of us think of a break as a stroke of good fortune, but we get bad breaks, too – and sometimes one comes disguised as the other. We all have setbacks, but no one point determines a win or loss. The lesson of "it bent but it didn't break" was that one should never give up because of a setback. No single event in life constitutes success or failure.

In a ping-pong match, it's the culmination of points that matters, the winner being the first to reach 21. Your game may start badly but end with a victorious flourish. You may rally for the win, whereas earlier your opponent had been piling up the points.

In wartime, the loss of one conflict doesn't mean the loss of the campaign. In fact, a defeat has often become a cause to fight on. "Remember the Alamo!" was the rally cry of Texans outraged at the Mexican siege at the mission. "Remember the *Maine!*" was the chant that precipitated the Spanish-American War after the battleship sank in Havana harbor.

Likewise, you may have a bad episode in your life and resolve never to go through that again. A divorce or a job loss might deliver you a blow, but you recover with a winning attitude, a renewed drive for success.

In many competitive sports, a player or team often overcomes a hard blow from the opponent – and that, in fact, is what makes the game exciting. The underdog can prevail.

Sometimes we come so close. Think of the golfer who misses a putt by inches. Or a basketball game that hangs on a final free throw – and the ball circles the rim, only to swing over the edge. Usually the loss doesn't ruin the season, the career, or the person. The same high level of skill and talent that produces victory can also result in a loss, so the players need not think of themselves as failures. And that's the attitude you must take in your pursuits.

"Come on," my father would tell me after winning a game of ping-pong, "that was only the first game of a best-of-three tournament, and there are many points still to play." He taught me to pick up my paddle and play again. And I learned that even in loss, one can learn valuable things about the competition. You get a sense for their strengths and weaknesses and strategies. You learn when to be cautious and when to take on risk, to push your advantage.

Each of us must determine our own acceptable level of risk. Our risk tolerance depends on our circumstances and our resources. For Donald Trump, a $100 million venture on a new building is a small risk; to somebody else, risking even $100 could put the month's rent payment in jeopardy. Some people are so introverted that it's an emotional risk to engage even one stranger in conversation; others are highly social yet still balk at the thought of giving a keynote address.

It's important, then, to be realistic and true to yourself – but remember that you likely will be at your best when you feel a bit of discomfort, as I did in that first golf shot I had in front of photographers. When I play golf with a complete novice, I tend not to do that well myself. But when I play with a pro, I instinctively give it my best. Surround yourself with people whose achievements you admire and wish to emulate, people who have attained "success" as you define it. Allow that inner circle to help fuel your inner fire.

The decisive factor, once again, is attitude. We influence the events in our lives by how we think about them. Those who try a new pursuit, or push themselves toward an accomplishment, with the attitude that they will learn and grow, regardless of success, are likely to prevail.

I think of a winning attitude as "the five L's," a good way to accept setbacks whether in a game or in business. They are *launch, lose, learn, leverage,* and *launch* again. You launch an idea, and you well may lose – but you learn, and you leverage what you learned into a greater understanding so that you can launch anew. That way, you transform any result into a lesson learned. Your break is the perspective you gain that allows you to interpret what happens positively.

So how can a bad break on the surface turn out to be a good break? Imagine someone getting into a car accident on the way to work. The car is totaled, and the driver breaks his arm. All in all, an awful day.

But at the hospital, a routine CAT scan finds something else lurking in the shadows of the tissue, something that has the potential to be so much worse. A skilled surgeon can help fix the problem, now that it has been identified, but it was the accident that saved this person's life. Without that one awful event, the growing menace likely would have gone undiscovered until it was too late. All in all, this was one of the best days of that person's life.

Events happen to all of us every day, both good and bad, and we all interpret them differently. Some add to our life, some subtract, and others are compounded and affect us profoundly, either negatively or positively. Think about your life and the most influential events that have shaped who you are today. Did they add, subtract, multiply or divide?

DETERMINE YOUR BREAK

How Do You Consider These Events
to Have Impacted Your Life?

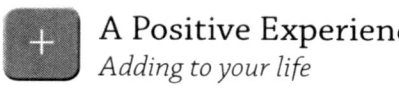 **A Positive Experience**
Adding to your life

 **A Negative Experience**
Detracting from your life

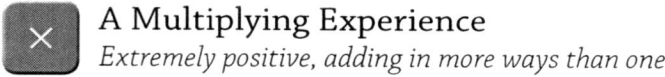 **A Multiplying Experience**
Extremely positive, adding in more ways than one

 **A Divisive Experience**
Extremely negative, pulling you away, causing separation

The Break Equation Analysis allows for introspection. It sets out to help you interpret your breaks in life and determine their true effect on you. Think about what's significant in your life. Many people would list their birth family, their marriage, their education, their financial scenario. You have to determine what the most significant events, or Break Factors, are in your life that have collectively shaped you – and the way you think. And you must examine how you have dealt with them, for that's what matters most.

By viewing a past experience in a new way, with a new perspective, you may not only free yourself of a prior inhibition but also you may give yourself the break you have been looking for all along.

\+ − × ÷

Let's start by defining some basic terms that we'll be using as we move forward in your personal journey through the Break Equation Analysis:

- **A Break Factor** is one of the top ten events in your life, both good and bad, that you determine to be most significant.

- **A Response Factor** is the numerical value, on a scale from -10 to +10 with zero being neutral, that you place on each Break Factor as you assess its significance in your life and, simply, how you feel about it.

- **A Break Score** is the value derived from the calculation, which will range from -10 to +10. It reflects not only the nature of events in your life but also, and most importantly, your attitude and reactions to them.

- **A Break Profile** is the story of someone's life, the breaks they have experienced, and how they have influenced their business ideas and aspirations.

We all have our own Break Profile already in life. But like our Break Score, it will continue to change as we experience more Break Factors along our journey in life. It is through the comparison of Breaking Profiles that we see that while the events, or Break Factors, in life may be common for so many of us, it is our individual reactions to those events, and the perspective we have on them, that differentiates us.

To start the Break Equation Analysis, which is available on our website (www.TheBreakEquation.com), you first must answer a series of questions – and you will be the one who chooses those questions. For some, this exercise may be quite difficult, particularly for those who have endured troubles and pain. But remember that nobody is judging your positives and negatives. The new perspective and understanding you gain will make your effort worthwhile.

As we bustle about day to day, it can be hard to pause and reflect on what it all means. We get good and bad breaks every day, big ones or small ones. We notice some; others we don't. Yet inevitably we reach a point where we wonder, "Why can't I catch a break?" or "Why do I always get the bad breaks?"

This is your opportunity to take that pause, to explore the Break Equation Analysis in order to gain a new perspective. That new mindset, along with the inspirational stories of other Breaking Profiles, will help to motivate you to action, action to take the next step in your career or on that business idea that you have been so eager to launch.

To start, then, you will determine your unique Break Factors. Set aside half an hour in a quiet and relaxing place. Listen to music, meditate, pray, or do whatever helps you to eliminate distractions. Invest these thirty minutes in yourself. Have a piece of paper with you.

Begin to think about your life, from your earliest memories to your latest meal. Think about the people you have known. Think of your career. Think of those events and experiences that have made you who you are. What do you recall?

If you need some help, here's a list of common events and situations that people often consider significant – not necessarily positive or negative, just significant. This can stimulate your thinking, but only you know the variables that belong in your Break Equation.

High school	First car	Your friends	Retirement
Religion	First job	Promotion	Serious illness
Your health	Loss of job	Getting engaged	Midlife crisis
Your family's health	Buying a house	Loss of a pet	College life
Your mother	Credit card debt	Conquering a fear	Adoption
Your father	High school prom	Starting a business	Bankruptcy
21st birthday	Broken heart	Major surgery	Infertility
First love	Work failure	Natural disasters	Realizing a dream
Driving a car	Divorce	Relocation	Playing an instrument
Travel	Violence	Getting arrested	Military service
Marriage	Becoming an aunt/uncle	Single parenthood	Being a best friend
Unemployment	Winning the lottery	Becoming a millionaire	Celebrity status
Growing old	Losing a bet	A big paycheck	Loss of a loved one
First airplane flight	Your age	Siblings	Your birth family

It can be hard to recall every detail, but certain moments and situations will stand out. Write them down. Don't worry about prioritizing or dwell on whether they were good or bad. For now, just brainstorm, without emotion. In those thirty minutes, jot down what comes to mind. You most likely will come up with a list of the most significant moments in your life.

Take some time to clear your head, and when you are ready, examine your list. You will see that much of what you put down amounts to good or bad breaks. They are positives and negatives in your life. Consider each one, asking yourself, "Was this a break for me in some manner?" If it was, keep it on the list. If not, remove it. Once you have the list of your top ten Break Factors you are ready to calculate your Break Score.

Go to www.TheBreakEquation.com and click on the "My Break Score" tab. The first step is to enter your list of ten Break Factors that you have just created. Each Break Factor will have a drop-down box with common examples that you can select if they apply to you, or you can type in entries from your personal list.

Once your list is complete, you are ready to evaluate each Break Factor. For each Break Factor that you have entered, you will see a sliding scale to the right with the mathematical symbols for addition, subtraction, multiplication and division.

Don't worry about the actual calculation – our system will do that for you. For now, at your own pace, begin to thoroughly examine each of your Break Factors so that you can assign the appropriate Response Factor to each one. You will be deciding whether a particular life experience was positive or negative, on a scale from +10 to -10, depending on whether it was a good break or a bad one, whether it added to your life or subtracted from it. If it is high on the positive scale, it likely had a multiplying effect on your life. If it is low on the negative scale, it likely had a divisive effect.

To help in your analysis, the following definitions will help you to better understand how to assign the best Response Factor for each Break Factor that you have identified.

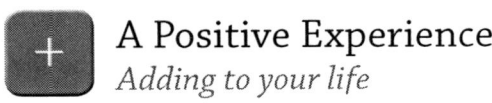 ## A Positive Experience
Adding to your life

- The Break Factor makes me smile when I think about it.

- The Break Factor helped me in life and was gratifying.

- The Break Factor can be considered a blessing, and I am thankful that it happened the way it did.

A **Positive Response Factor** has a numeric value of 1 to 5. You decide the level of emphasis. Consider 5 to be the greatest influence in this category.

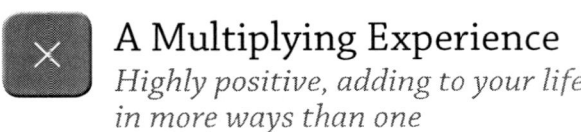 ## A Multiplying Experience
Highly positive, adding to your life in more ways than one

- The Break Factor makes me smile when I think about it. It changed my life for the better.

- The Break Factor helped me in life and was gratifying; it continued to influence other events and my emotions positively.

A **Multiplying Response Factor** has a numeric value of 6 to 10. You decide the level of emphasis. These Break Factors include life's best breaks. Consider 10 to be the greatest influence in this category.

A Negative Experience
Detracting from your life

- The Break Factor makes me sad or upset when I think about it.

- The Break Factor set me back in life emotionally, financially, or in other ways.

- The Break Factor was unfortunate; I was unlucky to have it in my life.

A **Negative Response Factor** has a numeric value of -1 to -5. You decide the level of emphasis. Consider -5 to be the most negative influence in this category.

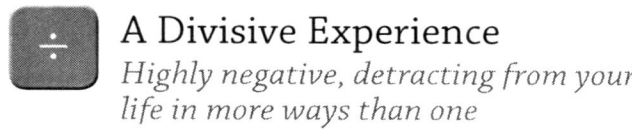
A Divisive Experience
Highly negative, detracting from your life in more ways than one

- The Break Factor makes me sad or upset when I think about it. It changed my life for the worse.

- The Break Factor set me back in life emotionally, financially, or in other ways.

- The Break Factor was unfortunate; I was unlucky to have it in my life and it continued to influence other events and my emotions negatively.

A **Divisive Response Factor** has a numeric value of -6 to -10. You decide the level of emphasis. These Break Factors include life's toughest breaks. Consider -10 to be the most negative in this category.

At this time, go through each of your Break Factors and assign a Response Factor value as you see fit. Be honest with yourself. For each, dig deep to determine how positive or negative it was for you. Only you will see the results, so make the most of this time. If you feel indifferent about a certain event, or decide it wasn't a break at all but just happened, assign a value of 0, and it will have a neutral effect on the evaluation. Take your time. There are no right or wrong answers. This is not a test; it's a personal investment in yourself and your future.

Again, don't worry about the actual calculation – our system will take care of that for you. As you will realize, it is quite simple and you can most likely calculate it by yourself. When you finish, simply click on "Calculate My Break Score" and you will be presented with your Break Score. You have now thoroughly investigated the most critical events in your life and evaluated how you feel about them. Congratulations!

Does it all seem too simple? That's a great question. The simplicity of the Break Equation Analysis reminds us how simple it can be to make a change in life if we so desire. The many small steps that we can make each and every day will eventually add up to significant change over time. However, the first requirement is a commitment from you to take action. For more analysis of the different Break Score results, visit us online at www.TheBreakEquation.com.

As you evaluate your Break Score, remember that it is a snapshot in time of how you feel about the most significant events in your life. It provides you an opportunity to reflect on how those feelings may be influencing other events or decisions. Your Break Score can change every day, or even every hour. And so can you.

Chapter 5:

KNOW THYSELF

My friend Bob lost a journalism job that he loved at *New York Newsday* years ago, when the newspaper abruptly closed. At the same time, his marriage was falling apart.

"It was just excruciating," he told me. "I figured life couldn't be anywhere near that bad ever again."

He didn't know what would become of his family – he had two small children, and it appeared he would have custody of them. He was intrigued by a job offer in Portland, Oregon, but it was withdrawn suddenly – not enough money in the newsroom budget. He felt frustrated at every turn – until the phone rang with a job offer in Philadelphia. Although happy to be employed, he struggled there financially as he raised his son and daughter. It seemed to be a lost decade.

Only years later did he come to understand that in truth it was a time of great beauty. He bonded with his children in a way that many men never do. For solace, he found a church – and a community of souls who showed him and his children the meaning of caring. Life was sweet, though he was lonely, and he often thought of the little farm where he had spent a happy boyhood. He longed to return to such a life.

And then he met a woman. She had escaped city poverty through hard work and wits and was running a horse farm out beyond the suburbs. She, too, was raising two children alone and lonely. She shared many of his dreams – and today, as husband and wife, they're living those dreams.

"If I hadn't lost that job," he said, sitting on the porch of their 18th-century stone house, "and if I hadn't ended up in Philadelphia with a broken marriage, I'd never have met her – and none of what we have now would have come to be. A lot of the joys that I have today would never have happened had it not been for the pain of fifteen years ago. People need to think about things like that."

Bob's score on the Break Equation Analysis showed him to have a high degree of optimism, an ability to see the best in things. I have a similar score. But had I met him on that day the newspaper closed – a day that he told me felt like a funeral – I doubt I could have consoled him with a pat on the back. I couldn't have reached him with, "Come on, Bob, it's going to be okay." He might even have found that annoying. But it was, indeed, okay. His worst day became his best.

Now that you've completed the evaluation, think about your own Break Score. Was it positive or negative?

If it was positive, you tend to have an optimistic attitude about the events in your life that you designate as most significant. Yes, perhaps you have been blessed to have experienced relatively few negative factors to date. It's more likely, however, that you've had your share of challenges but tend to see the bright side of life.

If your score was negative, you tend to have a pessimistic attitude about the events in your life that you deem most significant. It may be absolutely true that you have faced many troubles. However, they have influenced the way you think, driving feelings of defeat in a ripple effect. You tend to feel that you never get that break or you feel the cards are stacked against you.

For me, my Break Score was 7.4 when I went through the Break Equation Analysis. I like to think that reflects my Disney World mentality, as my friend sees it. I like to think I have a positive attitude, an optimism that drives my creativity and ambition. I hope my passion helps me to help others identify their own breaks and heed their call to action. But this is just me. A high score is not intrinsically better than a low score. It's all in what you make of it.

What did your Break Score tell you about yourself? Do you feel motivated to change anything in your life, or take any actions?

Regardless of where your score fell on the scale, let me again emphasize that it is only a snapshot of how you felt when you took the evaluation. Though it can help you to discover your prevailing attitude about life, your Break Score most likely will change if you take the evaluation on another day. Oenophiles know the subtle flavors that arise in a fine wine as it mellows over time. Your mood when you lift the glass – whether romantic, celebratory, pensive or jovial – also influences your perceptions. The taste of life is like that, too.

When you take the evaluation and see your Break Score, you are likely to reflect on what most impacted the results. This is normal to the process. You may conclude, for example, that you really have a more positive nature than the score indicates. You may then begin to rethink your attitude toward some of the events you listed.

Perhaps you didn't stop to consider how a positive experience truly helped others in a multiplying effect – and you'll want to increase that Response Factor. Perhaps you will realize that a negative you listed wasn't all that bad. You may even conclude that it was actually a positive – such as a job loss, or a divorce, that opened the door to greater fulfillment and happiness. Or that car accident that led to a CAT scan that uncovered a disease while it was still curable.

"Maybe I should think more positively," you might conclude. And if you were to take the evaluation again with that attitude, your Break Score likely would be significantly higher. *The Break Equation* encourages you to pause and reevaluate your life. You may discover something fundamental to the human experience: The pain of the past can be the blessing of the future.

Again, this is not a test. There is no right. There is no wrong. *The Break Equation* is not a critique of you in any way. People think and operate differently, and we need one another. Someone who has a high Break Score might do well to find a soul on the opposite spectrum to bring him or her back to earth, and someone with a low Break Score could benefit from a more optimistic perspective.

The Break Equation helps you to see that we all get breaks in many ways but often overlook them. It leads you to recalibrate your experiences as more positive influences that helped to make you who you are today.

Some things you cannot control. You can't choose the family into which you're born, for example. If you feel yours was a negative and continue to use that as an excuse for the shortcomings in your life, there comes a time when that blame must fall on you. Likewise, no one person can control the economy or the unemployment rate.

What you can control are your reactions. You can refuse to be defeated. You can resolve to take action, with ambition and creativity, and reach out to others. You can re-create yourself and try something new. There is nobody to hold responsible for your reactions, positive or negative, other than yourself.

Our life journey is a combination of the breaks that befall us and the ones that come at our behest. The latter play a major role, whether our reactions lead us to good breaks or bad ones. Just as we can turn a bad break into a good one, we can turn a good one to a bad. If you win millions in the lottery, for example, will you start a charitable foundation or will you become a paranoid money-grubber and die a friendless old Scrooge? Those who are given much in life have an opportunity to give much back.

Life deals each of us many of the same joys and struggles. Look back on the chart of common Break Factors in Chapter 4. Did any of the examples turn up on your own list? My guess is yes. If so many of us face the same events and experiences in life, how can it be that we end up so differently? Why does your neighbor seem healthier, happier, wealthier? Whether that neighbor is across the street or across the sea, we face universal experiences that transcend culture and tradition. We differ, however, in how we interpret and incorporate those experiences.

Through introspection and analysis, you can uncover trends. You can see how you have applied the four Response Factors and assess whether you have done so effectively. Then you can consciously change your responses to events to avoid common pitfalls and stay on course to a more fruitful, passionate life.

You need not wait for others or rely entirely on them. Yes, we all certainly need help along the way. But when you lay your head down on your pillow at night, it is only you who can envision how you will go about your next day. You have two options. One is to complain and envy others. Or you can embrace change.

Do you tell yourself you will be happy once you get to retirement? Or when the kids are out of school? When you lose twenty pounds, or get that job? Do you wish you had a shorter commute, a better boss, a new position? Do you want to live in a different town? Are you tired of debt and want more income?

It's time to create, not wait. Create your fulfillment now by finding the confidence to act. Instead of waiting for change to come to you, you can pursue it, moving forward without fear of failure or criticism. You could spend a lifetime just waiting – and life is short. Five years or even five minutes of waiting is precious time wasted.

Instead, look at the changes that already have come your way. Examine their significance, and think about how you reacted to them. You well may conclude that what you need more than a new break is a new way of thinking about the breaks you've already had. Have you turned bad ones into good ones? Have you squandered good ones? Has your quest for that one big break blinded you to your everyday fortunes? Do you endure the challenges in your life and yet learn nothing from them, with no lessons learned?

The time is now. There is happiness to be found, money to be made, and love to be discovered. There is no better time than now to reevaluate your life, embracing the good breaks that are multiplying and growing, and learning from those difficult ones. People and situations can bring us pain. The challenge is to find a way to understand, forgive, and turn negative energy into positive passion.

The Break Equation presents you with an opportunity to study yourself and your motivations so that you can make the most of life's opportunities. "Know thyself," Socrates said, "for that is the root of wisdom." "The unexamined life," he also declared, "is not worth living."

CHAPTER 6:

GIVE YOURSELF A BREAK

I'd like to share with you a Breaking Profile of the sort that has inspired me and speaks to many of the lessons of *The Break Equation*. Let me introduce you to Gene Johnson, whose remarkable story illustrates what we've been discussing about the nature of breaks and the passionate pursuit of opportunities. His story shows, above all, how we can give ourselves breaks by persevering with the right attitude.

+   −   ×   ÷

In the little town of Black River Falls, Wisconsin, 8-year-old Gene Johnson came in from play one day in 1948 to say he wasn't feeling well. It would be one of the most significant days of a most significant life.

For most of his young life, he had lived in rural farmhouses without indoor plumbing, using an outhouse and bathing weekly in a tub. His father hauled logs for a living. Though the family was poor, Gene didn't feel that way, and he had lots of friends.

On that memorable day in 1948, Gene was taken to the hospital, where he and his family received the stark diagnosis – polio. The next morning, Gene awoke and jumped out of bed, as all little boys are inclined to do – and fell flat on his face. His left leg was paralyzed.

The ensuing days were far from encouraging. One of the other children in his room – six children in each – was thought to be cured, but died soon after she was sent home. Her name was Mavis, and to this day Gene recalls his fear upon learning her fate.

Gradually, with physical therapy, Gene recovered some movement in his leg. However, even with this improvement, his muscles remained weak and he couldn't lift his left foot. At age 10, his parents took him to Milwaukee for surgery to correct the foot. Although he was in a cast, on many days he had to walk two miles to school on crutches through the snow.

In time, he recovered enough to play sports and participate in most activities. Compared to poor Mavis, he had been quite fortunate.

Gene's high-school days in Black River Falls were much like anywhere else in small-town U.S.A. He hung out with good friends, and sometimes they'd take the train to Milwaukee to see a baseball game. There wasn't much trouble to get into, though sometimes they skipped school or had a few beers.

His closest friend was a guy named Jon, son of a prominent businessman. Jon's dad would offer guidance that would prove to be a very positive break for Gene. To have more opportunity in life, Gene realized, he'd eventually have to leave Black River Falls.

When Gene graduated from high school, his mother gave him $300 and wished him good luck. Gene left for Madison,

Wisconsin, to work as a billing clerk for Consolidated Freightways. He also enrolled at Madison Business College with the right intentions, but left after a year to chase other passions.

He started hitchhiking to California. In Ames, Iowa, running out of money, he stopped at the police station and asked to spend the night. The police let him stay in a cell and gave him breakfast.

Arriving in Pasadena at age 18, he hooked up again with Consolidated Freightways. Wisconsin seemed so far away. One morning, he heard on the radio that the nation's coldest temperature had been recorded at 50 below zero – in Black River Falls.

He enrolled in a few classes at Pasadena City College but was still uncertain what he wanted to do with his life. He had been in California about a year when he read in the paper about a volunteer organization that President Kennedy was starting called the Peace Corps.

It was a Saturday, but Gene got on the phone to call the Peace Corps headquarters in Washington. Somehow he got connected with a deputy director, and they chatted for an hour.

"Gene, if you can be in Washington next Saturday, I'd be happy to meet with you," the official told him. Gene packed up his Volkswagen and drove cross-country for the next five days. At the meeting, Gene learned that training would begin Monday at Purdue University for a group going to Chile. He sold his car and belongings for a plane ticket to Lafayette, Indiana, and two weeks of intensive training in Spanish and Chilean history.

At Purdue, Gene met George, another trainee, who would eventually be the best man at his wedding. After Purdue they went to Puerto Rico for more training in survival techniques, language and culture.

Six of his fellow trainees were sent home. They hadn't made the cut. Those chosen had one week before leaving, so Gene returned to California to be with friends and family.

En route to Chile, the group had to fly around Cuba. It was 1962, during the missile crisis. The flight took nineteen hours. Finally arriving in Santiago, they saw the headline in the local communist paper: *45 American Spies Arrive in Chile.*

Gene was sent to the Chiloé Archipelago in southern Chile to work for a year with the Institute of Rural Education at a school serving about fifty local girls. They were 16 to 21 years old, and Gene was 19. For many reasons, he enjoyed the school and the work very much. However, it was chilly and rained almost every day. Charles Darwin spent about a month on the archipelago, and in his book *Voyage of the Beagle* said he'd never been so glad to leave a place in his life.

The Peace Corps experience shaped Gene's life. Though he and his colleagues aided Chile's development, most of them benefited individually as much or more by experiencing another culture. Gene left the United States as a Kennedy Democrat and returned as a conservative Republican. While in Chile, he read *Atlas Shrugged* by Ayn Rand. It changed his outlook on life. He realized that if you want something bad enough, you have to work for it – there is no such thing as a free ride.

Gene left Chile in 1964 and, with a fellow Peace Corps volunteer, took a cruise ship to Spain. It took 17 days. The ship was filled with young people who had been studying in Buenos Aires and were returning home to Spain and Italy. After living two months on the beach in Spain, Gene felt ready to return to the United States.

He got back in time for the 1964 presidential elections between Goldwater and Johnson. Peace Corps volunteers were by and large quite liberal and backed Johnson, so Gene put together a group called "Ex-Peace Corps Volunteers for Goldwater." There were only five in his group, he recalls. Goldwater lost in a landslide.

He then moved to New York City where he talked his way into a job as a financial analyst with AIG Corp. His colleagues there were quite impressed with his background in the Peace Corps. He stayed with AIG about two years, then switched to Bristol-Myers, also as a financial analyst. He was good with numbers and received three promotions in two years. He was on a fast track until politics got in the way.

In 1967, he volunteered to work on the Nixon campaign. Nixon's opponent in the Republican primary was Nelson Rockefeller. At the Republican Convention, Gene met staffers including Rockefeller's campaign manager, R. Burdell Bixby. That contact would soon prove to be a significant break in Gene's life.

Seeing Gene's potential, the campaign team asked him to be an advance man, traveling around the United States doing advance work for Nixon and Agnew. After Nixon won the election, most of Gene's campaign friends moved to Washington to be part of the new administration. Gene, however, returned to work at Bristol-Myers. He liked New York City.

In 1969, Rockefeller was gearing up his campaign to run for reelection as New York governor. Bixby recommended that Rockefeller bring Gene on as his director of advance work and scheduling operations. Rockefeller wrote to Dick Gelb, the CEO of Bristol-Myers, asking if Gene could be granted a six-month leave of absence to work on his campaign. Those six months turned into two years.

After spending so much time in politics, Gene and his wife, whom he'd married in 1967, decided to give Washington a try. Having worked on the Nixon campaign, it was easy for him to get a political position.

Gene decided to work at the Postal Service, which was in the process of changing from a government agency into a quasi-private operation. This decision would be yet another turning point in his life as it was at the Postal Service where he learned all about mail – and the future of e-mail.

Gene was in charge of developing advanced mail services and was involved in the development of the first e-mail service called Mailgram, which was a joint venture with Western Union. During his time there, Gene went on to develop several cutting edge hybrid electronic mail services which included Facsimile Mail Service and E-COM, which stood for electronic computer originated mail.

Gene had several job offers in private industry because of his work in electronic mail. In 1980, he joined ITT Corporation, working on developing business opportunities. He was responsible for the acquisition of one of the leading e-mail companies at the time called Dialcom.

A close friend, Bill Von Meister, had started a venture called Control Video and tried to get Gene to have ITT invest in it. Gene and Bill had worked together on developing Mailgram, when Bill was a consultant for Western Union. Gene told him he didn't think there was a market for his service, but Bill was persistent. Finally, Gene agreed to meet with Bill and a few new people he said had become involved in the project, including a man named Jim Kimsey. However, ITT declined to make the investment.

The company later changed its name to AOL, with Kimsey becoming chief executive officer. For a $5 million investment, ITT could have owned 20 percent of the firm that later would have been involved in a multibillion merger with Time Warner. Gene had made a mistake, a negative break in his life. In retrospect, ITT certainly should have made that investment.

Still, by 1986, at the age of 45, he had learned a lot about finance at AIG and Bristol-Myers, about e-mail while at the Postal Service, and about business development while at ITT. It provided him with a good background for launching his next career as an entrepreneur.

Gene left ITT in 1986 with an idea – one that he may never have pursued if the AOL deal had happened. He had been thinking about it since his years at the Postal Service.

He wanted to develop a hybrid electronic mail service. A business could send mail from its computer electronically to strategically located print sites around the United States. The objective was to reduce costs and improve service. He called the new business venture TCOM, which stood for terminal computer originated mail.

Gene had a few thousand dollars in the bank and thought he could get funding for the venture within three months. He recruited a first-class management team, including Bill Bolger, his old boss at the Postal Service, as chairman; and Bob Ryan, founder of Dialcom, as president and CEO.

Bob and Gene focused on raising money, meeting with various organizations over the first six months with no success. Quickly, Gene was down to his last thousand dollars in the bank.

He had a wife, two children, and a mortgage. The pressure was mounting.

Then one day the phone rang. It was John May, at the time a small venture capital player who later became very well known for putting several Angel groups together for investment purposes. He said he would put $50,000 into the venture. Everything had just changed. Targeting small investors, primarily friends and family, they raised $1.5 million within three months.

In the next six months they raised the $25 million more they felt they needed to fully develop the network. Investors included several of the major financial and insurance companies. They closed on the financing in October of 1987, the Friday before the infamous "Black Monday" when the U.S. stock market lost 25 percent of its value. Had his deal not closed on that Friday, the financial world would have looked very different in only a few days. A little luck and timing certainly never hurts.

However, even with that stroke of good fortune, it was within two years that they had lost all the money invested in the company. The reason for the failure was that the technology had not reached the point where it needed to be in order for the concept and company to be successful.

Gene felt bad for the many friends, including his good friend from his childhood days growing up in Wisconsin, who lost their investment. The next months were very difficult, as you can imagine, and Gene stayed busy working as a consultant as he came to terms with the failure of TCOM, and the lessons learned.

While frustrated, the ideas did not stop coming and his confidence to try again was not shaken. In 1991, he decided to start another e-mail company. The technology had improved and he thought that he had learned from his mistakes. Raising $1 million from a Washington-based company, he started Business Mail Express with a good management team.

The company was fairly successful, and Gene sold the company to some New York investment bankers for $20 million in 1993. He continued with the company for a couple of years and left in 1995, still yearning for "the big break."

For the next couple of years he put together a plan for his next venture. He thought the technology had improved to the point where an email company with a nationwide network of print locations could be very successful. Feeling yet another call to action, he called the company Mail2000, and he would need about $10 million to develop and implement the network.

Gene and business partner Paul Carlin, a former postmaster general, were in Europe on a trip and Gene suggested to Paul that they get in touch with some people from TPG, which is the Dutch Post Office in Holland, because the Dutch were very aggressive in looking at the future of electronic mail services at the time.

Through persistence, they set up an initial meeting in Chicago. The TPG team was impressed with the venture and invited them back to Amsterdam. Within eight weeks, the Dutch signed a deal for $10 million in venture money for 30 percent of the equity in the company.

They began service in 2000, bringing in major customers. Gene decided to bring on a major strategic partner based in the United States. He contacted a major parcel provider and made a presentation to their executive management team.

The parcel company liked the idea but was reluctant to get involved because TPG was one of its competitors in the international market. However, they agreed to form a joint venture and buy the management team out of the company. Just a few days before closing on that agreement, however, TPG and the parcel company had a falling out. With approximately $100 million at stake, Gene asked what it would take to save the deal. The parcel company said it would need to own the entire company. Gene flew to Amsterdam, and TPG reluctantly agreed to sell its share. TPG had made $30 million on a $10 million investment that it had held for 14 months. Not a bad return.

After selling Mail2000, Gene was under contract to work for the company for another two years. During those years and for several years thereafter, Gene and his wife, Livia, whom he credits as critical to his success, had the opportunity to travel extensively, visiting many amazing places around the world.

Gene and Livia were now financially comfortable, yet he continued to think of and search for the next big venture. After all, that was his passion. He liked to call the idea of his next venture his "Gulf Stream V," or GSV, project. A GSV, an executive luxury aircraft, costs about $55 million, and he would need a big hit, or break, to buy this type of plane. It would make life easier traveling around the world and back to their home in Puerto Vallarta, Mexico.

At the time this book was published, Gene was launching a new business venture, believing in his uniquely optimistic way in its potential to become one of the biggest internet-related company in the world, and he remains involved in several other endeavors. He continues to follow his passions.

Gene's civic and volunteer work throughout his journey also reflects his commitment to sharing the good fortune of the breaks he has had in life. He has served on two presidential boards and commissions; one was responsible for writing the Americans with Disabilities Act, and the other was the Peace Corps advisory board. He was also chairman of Rebuilding Together, which rehabs houses around the United States. The houses are for elderly people or people with disabilities who don't have the means to rehab their homes.

Gene has met many people on his journey to date, and quite a few have been instrumental in his success. He certainly doesn't take that for granted. And now, with the next chapter of his life under way, one thing that certainly can be taken for granted is that his nightstand notes are always full. Gene has two sons who have grown to follow in his footsteps. They have learned that one can never accept failure but always learn something from it as they continue to follow their own passions and red wine wishes.

+   −   ×   ÷

Each day that we are alive presents another opportunity, with options and avenues for us to consider. How will we react to the next moment of adversity? Will we give up and lose confidence, or will we persevere? This is a choice we all must make regularly. Gene has known this since his early days with polio. He made up his mind that he would thrive, and he pursued one break after another with passion and confidence.

For many of us, life's decisions seem like a coin toss. We may not always see clearly the right path forward. Yet we want results and seek guidance and direction. So we flip a virtual coin and move forward with the repercussions of the decision. Sometimes life seems as happenstance as that.

When you flip that coin, it has a 50/50 chance of landing either way, leading you potentially to a good break or a bad break. You can't control how that coin lands, but you can control how you react to the result. It's easy to react well to a good break and equally easy to look for excuses when things don't turn out the way you had hoped. For example, have you ever heard "I didn't have the money" or "it just wasn't my time" or "luck never comes my way"?

At one time or another, most all of us have used the excuse, "I just don't have the time." The reality is that we all have plenty of time, day in and day out, for what we establish as priorities. Are your priorities only what you feel you have to do? Or do you include what you want to do?

We lean on so many excuses.

But there is no excuse for an excuse. It's time to be honest with yourself about what is important in your life, what you want to do, what you want to spend time on, and then focus on that. Have the confidence to share that mission and priority with others. If you don't do it soon and keep making those excuses, I question whether it is something you actually intend to do – and so should you. If that's the case, revisit your idea at some later date and just stop talking about it.

The point is this: Focus on what you intend to do and not what sounds like the right thing to say. The next time someone tells you about a great business venture or invention that could make millions, ask that person when he or she last spent two hours actually working to make it happen. It well could be that you'll find a lack of confidence – all talk without action. It is far better to concede lack of interest than to use excuses as a cover. Be true to yourself.

When you make an excuse, you are trying to solicit sympathy from others, hoping they will say, "The cards were certainly stacked against you" or "You were stuck in the position you were in." You may feel temporary relief, but you don't move forward at all. The excuse doesn't go away, and now you may feel you have to live behind it.

If you fall into that category, as many of us do at times, it is important to focus on your priorities and stop those excuses. Say to yourself that you are going to leave your comfort zone and go after a dream, a vision, a passion. You may not succeed, but you are taking action. As Gene Johnson would surely acknowledge, your first few ventures may well fall short. But you are on your way.

We all have red wine wishes. We all harbor ambitions and desires – to open a great restaurant, to write the screenplay for a blockbuster movie, to travel to a far-off land, to volunteer for a cause that makes a difference. Since we all have such ambitions, we can build upon them by sharing the excitement.

At some point, however, you need to give yourself a break – that is, you need to move beyond talking and take action. Your wishes cannot become reality unless they go from nightstand note to daytime deed. Someone picked up the first chisel to start building Rome, and after many days it was done. You, too, can start with small steps toward your goal. Your passion will grow along the way.

Failure to act indicates lack of confidence and a fearful attitude. You need not fear failure. Your honest attempt is what reflects your passion, not whether you succeed. Failure provides you with a lesson upon which to build success, and you may need to fall short more than once to figure out what to do differently.

If you should make your fortune, it's okay to strive for more – so long as you don't take it for granted. So many people rest on their success, feeling they have tried enough or don't need to reach new levels. I believe an obligation of successful people is to share their experience, time, or resources to foster success in others.

One also must take care not to rest on the success of others. Do you know of people who float through life, without passion, resting on the accomplishments of those who came before them? They abuse a blessing instead of honoring its source by working hard and channeling the resources wisely. They could be helping others, just as they have been helped.

In such instances, having a safety net in life may stifle ambition. It can blind some people to the day-to-day breaks they receive. If they have dreams, they never get around to acting on them because they simply don't feel the urgency. Having all the money you need might seem like one of life's most precious breaks – and it could indeed be so. But it can also be a bad break, even divisive, if it stifles your passion and ambition to step outside your comfort zone and make your own contribution, on top of those blessings from those who came before.

For Gene, the millions he made later in life changed his lifestyle for certain. However, it did not make him happier than when he was on that ship headed for Europe with his buddies. He was just as rich then, though not in material wealth. True success came from knowing he was on his way. You are happy when you are fulfilling your passions.

When my father was in medical school, he and my mom would often order a seven-dollar pizza and have a few couples over for dinner and to play cards. Later, when he could afford more, they would go into New York City for fancy dinners easily costing over $200. "I was just as happy having that seven-dollar pizza," he told me once.

That underscores a principle of *The Break Equation:* It is not just about financial gain. That can be one wonderful result. But more important is the passion. More important is taking chances rather than just talking or complaining. More important is taking action.

I hate hearing how people dislike their jobs, their commute, their financial scenario, and the politics of their workplace, yet continue down that path year after year. They may exude confidence about their steady job, but do they in truth fear the risk of failure if they were to try something different?

Success at one pursuit or occupation doesn't make you a success overall, especially if you are ignoring your dreams. Likewise, you are not a failure just because one venture didn't make it. If you were true to yourself, you were a winner, because win or lose, you learned.

I'm sure you've heard this definition of insanity: Doing the same thing repeatedly, yet expecting a different result. If you keep flipping a coin hoping that it will lead you to your big break, you are leaving your life to chance.

Instead, you can make your own break. Don't wait for it to come your way. Make it happen. Get creative. Take a chance. Be willing to fail. Refuse to fail to act. If you think you've had a bad break, change the game. When you have a good break, multiply it.

Let me show you a new kind of coin, the Break Equation Coin. It's an unusual one. It has neither heads nor tails. Instead, each side is a mirror. When you peer down to see the results of your latest flip, you will see only yourself gazing back. Either way your fortune falls, what will matter most is *you*.

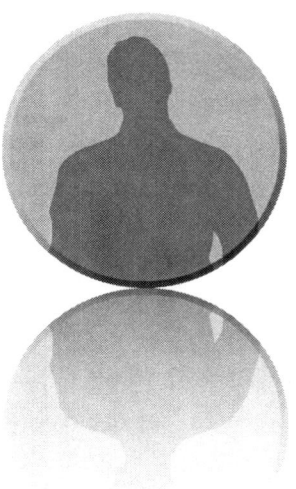

Go ahead and flip that Break Equation Coin. Did you get the result that you were seeking? You may see that it reflects many breaks you didn't recognize you had. You may also see in your reflection some bad breaks that you overcame and turned to good – the way Samantha did.

As we store away our many life experiences, we create a valuable bank of lessons. If you keep them to yourself, only you will benefit. But if you share those lessons, you can help to guide others and enrich their lives. If you are willing to give yourself a break, you need not stop there: You can help others get their break, too.

CHAPTER 7 :

A TAP ON THE SHOULDER

You can learn so much from a game of checkers.

My mother's father, Charles, was a man of Austrian descent. We used to call him Oopa. When I was a little boy, Oopa played many roles: He was my never-ending source of Pepperidge Farm Bordeaux cookies, a loyal patron of my $5 car washes in the driveway, and a worthy opponent in a game of checkers.

Oopa's visits to our house on Tuesday nights seemed as certain as sunrise and sunset. My mother, Nancy, made dinners of beef stroganoff, followed by apple pie with vanilla ice cream. We'd cap the day with the evening news and an episode of *Wheel of Fortune*, and often we would sit down at the checker board.

Oopa had been a banker, working at Chase Manhattan Bank in New York City for many years. From the many stories I have heard about his career, I know that he had a great work ethic and an elegant, professional style, wearing a three-piece suit every day. He had an adventurous spirit, enjoying frequent day trips and voyages to faraway places.

Life changed for him with the early passing of his wife, my grandmother Eleanor, when she was only 49. As a child, I wasn't aware of his pain and what he had endured. I also didn't know my grandfather as the banking executive or the adventurous traveler. To me, his only travels seemed to be to our house for those Tuesday night dinners.

Who was the grandfather I knew? I remember his hugs. I remember "Honeybun," his nickname for me and my sister, Elizabeth. I remember his hello and goodbye kisses, always accompanied by three or four pats on the face. They were his hallmark. Elizabeth and I would regularly reenact them – though my version was more like a smack, which got me in trouble with our mom and dad. To this day, we both still remember this expression of love vividly.

Oopa's gentle pats could almost bowl you over; such was the power and passion of his love for family as I could feel it as a little boy. I can still feel it today. I close my eyes and find myself in the kitchen of our childhood home, and I'm 8 years old again. I can smell his sweater. He smiles at me. We're finishing dinner, and Oopa gets up to get a toothpick, his napkin still tucked into his belt. At bedtime, my sister and I run to him for hugs. "Goodnight, Honeybun," I hear once again. And Oopa pats my cheek.

While Mom was fixing dinner in the kitchen, Oopa would settle into the couch in our living room to watch the CBS evening news with Dan Rather. I would try my best to persuade him to watch something more exciting such as *Three's Company*, *Diff'rent Strokes*, or *Family Ties*.

"Let Oopa watch his news," my mother would call in from the kitchen. "You get going on your homework."

My mother worked so hard to make those Tuesday evenings special – and today she continues the tradition with her grandchildren. After all, she says, "it's still all about family." I know that it was my mother's dedication and love that allowed us to get to know our Oopa so well.

As he got ever older and his hearing failed, the TV volume would slowly rise over the course of the night. One of my jobs would be to go upstairs and get the other remote control, sneak down to the adjacent room, and secretly lower the volume to a manageable level. Oopa usually did not detect it right away, but by *Jeopardy!* time at 7:30, the TV would be loud again.

Oopa always was willing to play checkers as we watched TV together. As you probably know, when a checker player's piece reaches the far side of the board, it is crowned and becomes a king. One of the pieces that had been captured, and had been set aside, defeated only for a time, is then used as that crown, making the king stand twice as tall, more powerful than ever and ready to redouble his efforts to win the game.

As Dan Rather reported the news and the TV volume blared, I felt that I had a distinct advantage, as Oopa would be paying more attention to the events of the day than to the next strategic checkers move. And to me, the game did appear to be one of great strategy. I'll never forget the joy of crowning my kings. I recall having this experience with unusual frequency, leading me to believe, in retrospect, that my Oopa's guiding hand helped my "strategy."

Something similar happened when I played stickball with my dad on our driveway. As you may recall from my earlier story, he was a former high school baseball star. I was a short 8-year-old – yet somehow, game after game, we would find ourselves tied in extra innings, bottom of the eleventh, and I would finally hit a home run over the neighbor's fence in left field to win the game.

Could I possibly have been the better baseball player and the ultimate checkers champion? I wasn't sure at the time, and I rarely thought about whether they were letting me win. I would just ask to play again – best two out of three.

I couldn't get enough of hanging out and playing with my grandfather and my dad. And I know now, from the perspective of years passing, that each of those men was trying to teach me something far more important than the rules of the game.

I often think back on those checkers games, those dinners, and that happy household. My sister and I were innocently unaware then of life's troubles that had changed our grandfather. Today I find myself wondering what he was like when he was young, in love, and starting out.

I wish I could have dinner again with my Oopa – and I don't mean a Tuesday stroganoff with the old man. I would like to share a table with a 25-year-old Charles. I'd like to hear his dreams. I want him to share his excitement about all the breaks he anticipated. I want him to tell me his red wine wishes.

Many nights as I fall asleep, I do find myself at dinner with him. He looks the way I remember him, as an older man, and his smile is the same. But as we talk, his perspectives are those of a young man. He shares with me his passions, his daydreams, his ambitions – yet, he still pats my cheek as we say farewell. I like to think with pride that I take after my Oopa in many ways.

I understand now what those loving pats revealed about the man he was and the breaks he gave to me and our family. I understand, too, what you can learn from a game of checkers. He played quietly, methodically, as he considered his moves with what I believe was one overriding strategy: to make me feel like a king.

My grandfather knew that if I could feel like a king while playing checkers, I would feel like one in life.

I didn't recognize this lesson, or break, at the time we were playing checkers – I was just being a kid, enjoying time with my grandfather. With age and with time, and with a new perspective of *The Break Equation,* I have come to appreciate even more the many lessons he imparted in his own way and the multiplying impact of the breaks he gave to us in life.

You certainly can learn a lot from a game of checkers.

+   −   ×   ÷

Over the past 15 years, I have often been reminded of my grandfather's pats on the face as I've experienced encouragement and support from others. It's called, in corporate America, the "tap on the shoulder," and though it doesn't come with the affection that Oopa bestowed, it does carry this message: "I believe in you."

It works like this: You're walking down the office hall one day or leaving the cafeteria when an executive taps your shoulder. There's a new position, it seems, or a special project, or an extra task of utmost importance that seems perfect for you. Are you up to it? The only answer is "yes."

This is the corporation's way of saying, "We are confident that you can handle more responsibility."

Many of us may wait for such a tap, and often it does come. But for others, through no fault of their own, that tap may never come, or it may simply not come when we are looking for one, or needing one.

How is a corporation to know what you are capable of? Yes, you give it your all for eight hours or more each day, but rarely do you have the opportunity to share your life's passions.

When that tap on the shoulder comes, you are thrust into a world of activities focused on the specific needs of the individual or department that chose you for the challenge. But consider whether that focus is one you are passionate about. Do you want to be the chair of this new department? Do you want to lead the new hiring initiative? Do you want to manage the reorganization of the marketing department? These responsibilities will take a lot of your time – but whose ambitions do they advance – yours, or the one who tapped your shoulder? Are you merely doing a task someone else doesn't want to do?

I don't mean to sound like a skeptic here. I've had my shoulder tapped, and I felt proud when it happened – and I still do. It is a sign that you are respected within the organization.

However, you don't need to go to the office every day waiting for that tap on the shoulder. Tap yourself on the shoulder tonight at 5:01 p.m. when you leave the office. Give yourself the responsibility of controlling your destiny and acting on that dream you wrote down on a nightstand note a few weeks back. Put your career on the path you desire. Day by day, you will see more clearly whether a tap on the shoulder leads you farther along that path or pulls you away from it.

I like to think my Oopa's loving pat on the cheek was one of the early encouraging taps that I received in life, with the message that anything was possible and that he believed in me, win or lose. It was filled with confidence that I could not only win at checkers but also that I could win at life. Such confidence allows you to encourage yourself, with perfect timing that's not on someone else's clock.

+   −   ×   ÷

I know that I am where I am today because of the love and support of those who are ahead of me in the journey of life, those who believed in me and gave me my earliest breaks. That includes my parents, grandparents, and so many others – as well as previous generations that I never had the opportunity to know.

I believe we all strive to leave the next generation better off than the previous one. I don't like to think of it as giving back in life but rather as paying it forward. This happens in small acts of day-to-day love and support that, over time, makes a cumulative difference in the lives of those around us. I have been fortunate to experience such a multiplying break, and I strive to do my best in order to do the same for those in my life today.

In the business world, companies also try to do this by leaving the next generation of leaders more prepared to lead, more prepared to make a positive difference in society. In my filing cabinet, I have a few ideas that I hope to someday incorporate into my endeavors in the years ahead.

For example, I once created an idea called Next Generation Leadership. Built around a concept similar to the hit reality show *Survivor*, this business would include *Survivor*-type outings for corporations and executive teams. The outings would help to build leadership, strengthen teams, and encourage networking.

Experienced leaders would share their savvy with those destined to take their place.

Also stored away is an idea called "How Much Does a Smile Cost?" a charitable program that would foster appreciation for the value of a simple smile. I have a great respect for organizations such as Smile Train and Operation Smile. In short, they provide time, money, and resources to work with people in developing countries where there are millions of children suffering with unrepaired clefts. A cleft lip is a congenital deformity of the top part of the lip and a cleft palate is a more serious deformity involving the hard palate, or roof of the mouth. I was born with a cleft lip. Today, a cleft lip or palate can be successfully treated with surgery, especially so if conducted soon after birth or in early childhood.

However, in these developing countries, many children continue to suffer – and they simply cannot easily smile. Most of these children would do anything for that simple pleasure we take for granted. I admire the work that these organizations do, along with so many other organizations focused on helping those less fortunate fulfill their dreams. By helping others, I believe we all can find our own fulfillment along the way. If you pay it forward, it will come back to you in ways you might never have imagined.

Many of us, unfortunately, take our good fortune for granted – and that's what I did when I was a child, after my cleft lip was repaired. I soon forgot how lucky I was to be able to smile. Life has a way, however, of sending gentle reminders. In college, I was diagnosed with Bell's palsy, a condition that is marked by a rapid onset of partial or complete facial paralysis that often occurs overnight, resulting from a dysfunctional cranial, or facial, nerve. Within hours, I was unable to control the facial muscles on the affected side. With medical treatment and time, my facial function returned to normal, however, that is not always the case.

With time and perspective, I am certain that the episode of Bell's palsy, though frightening, was a positive break in my life: I was reminded once again about the simple pleasure of smiling. It reminded me of how much money could be raised for charity if people donated a penny every time someone's smile made them feel a little better – or perhaps made them smile themselves. As I think back on my experiences with a cleft lip and Bell's palsy, I'm continually reminded of these bad breaks turned good in my life and equally motivated to continue to find ways to share that good fortune with others.

I challenge you now to pay it forward, and I hope *The Break Equation* has given you the understanding and inspiration to do so. Perhaps you can help your son or daughter, or your spouse, or a colleague – or even a stranger that you meet.

Take the time to ask people about their mission and passions in life, even as you work to develop your own. Tell them how you found a way, and help them to know they can do it, too. We could make a huge difference if we each encouraged even one person a year to find success and fulfillment – someone with the right heart, mind, and passions, but who has yet to find the confidence to change.

Offer those would-be dreamers whatever you can: A few dollars, perhaps, or a few words of encouragement. Suggest a good book to read, a good class to take, or someone they simply must meet. Maybe a pat on the back would work best. Or just a smile. After all, how much does a smile cost?

CONCLUSION:

NOW IS YOUR MOMENT

My hope is that you have taken time to evaluate your life and its milestones and how you have reacted to them. I hope you have concluded that anything is possible. Tonight, perhaps, you will wake up with a new dream and jot down a new nightstand note.

Promise yourself to do something about that dream. Don't wait for the right moment or some grand idea. Start small but start now. As we have learned, confident steps and simple gestures can have multiplying effects for you and the world around you.

Remember that your Break Score today will be different tomorrow, changing like that bottle of red wine, so revisit your calculation from time to time. Calculate your Break Score when you are in a good mood and when you are in a bad mood, during the day and again at night. Perhaps by seeing just one Break Factor in a different light, with a new perspective, you can free yourself of a prior inhibition and gain the confidence to once again follow your dreams. You will see clearly that your Break Score can change, and you can use that insight itself as a positive break — because what it means, in essence, is that you, too, can change. Your fate is never sealed.

Whether your breaks thus far have been good or bad, you can be sure that more of both lie ahead. Embrace the good ones and learn from the bad ones. By enduring, we grow. As the author J.K. Rowling once said: "It is impossible to live without failing at something, unless you live so cautiously that you might as well not have lived at all."

Life will send you sweet breezes and storms. But the lesson here bears repeating: It's not what life deals you — it's how you deal with life.

In his book *How We Decide*, science journalist Jonah Lehrer investigated how the human mind makes decisions. He told of experiments done by a researcher at the University of Bordeaux in which wine aficionados were invited to a unique wine tasting.

In one experiment, the wine lovers were given a white wine dyed red. They described the scent of blackberries and tannins and the qualities of the crushed red fruit. They were served table wine, poured from an expensive bottle. They talked of its refinement, its elegance.

It's not at all about trickery or gullibility. The point is this: The mind meets our expectations. We see and taste what we hope to see and taste. It's all in how we look at it. It's the human way.

That means it's your way, too. It's time to understand all those breaks in life, the good ones and the not-so-good, that have defined who you are. Embrace your dreams. Have faith in those nightstand notes you jot down long past midnight. Flip your Break Equation Coin, and know that you are in control of the course your life takes. You need not wait any longer to pursue those red wine wishes. Now is your moment.

APPENDIX:

ABOUT THE BREAK EQUATION WEBSITE

(www.TheBreakEquation.com)

So, are you ready to catch a break and chase that big idea from dream to reality? The first step is to start your own ignition. In fact, you may have already done so by reading this book. We hope you have found in it the key to get you started.

Now, we encourage you to visit us online at www.TheBreakEquation.com. By evaluating your Break Score, you will see that while we all receive both good and bad breaks in life, it is not so much the events themselves but rather our reactions to them that matters most. From there, when you are ready, take the call to action on your passion, your emerging business idea, at the Break Equation Incubator.

As we read in *The Break Equation*, the stories of people like Samantha and Gene show us that anything is possible. And now it is your turn. Perhaps you want to open a restaurant, or buy a franchise, or make a movie. You have certain strengths to accomplish these dreams, but you may not have all that it takes. Few of us do and recognizing that we may need some help is a big positive break in itself.

For example, perhaps you want to run a bed-and-breakfast but you only have one piece of the dream – you own a delightful vintage house in a tourist town. Outside of that, you don't know where to begin. That doesn't mean you are not able to act on your dream. You can look for a partner who shares your passion, who knows how to set up this business, and maybe even likes to cook.

The Break Equation Incubator is made up of a team of people who have a passion for helping to bring dreams to reality. Think of this portion of the Break Equation Incubator as a dream incubator, where we strive to bring people and resources together in order to help bring your ideas, your nightstand notes, to life.

So, how does it work? Our team of Break Advisors will be reviewing the business idea submissions received at the Break Equation Incubator from you, our Breaking Profiles, to select a few that catch our eye. For those that do, we will be contacting you to discuss what skills, resources, mentoring, and support you may need in order to help bring that dream and passion to reality.

Like the Break Equation Analysis, our goal is simple: To use *The Break Equation* tools to help to bring at least one reader's passion to reality, to help multiply the good that can come from one person giving him or herself a break and taking the call to action on their business idea. And we hope that person is you.

And if it is, we hope you pay it forward and return the favor to someone with a business idea and passion that catches your eye by being their mentor, their personal Break Advisor. In doing so, day-by-day, over time, this community of Breaking Profiles will be individually, small step after small step, making a big difference.

> - A Genuine Passion
> - A Creative Business Idea
> - A Positive Can-Do Attitude

What YOU Promise

> - A Genuine Passion
> - A Creative Business Infrastructure to Help Your Idea
> - A Positive Can-Do Attitude

What WE Promise

Regardless of the stage of your idea or depth of your resources, we are proud that you have taken this confident next step with your business idea. While we certainly can't promise that your idea will become the next Google, we hope the Break Equation Incubator serves as a spark to help you bring your dream to reality.

+ − × ÷

How can you get started today?

Life is often about following our intuition, or gut feeling. The same is true of innovation. Do you have a strong gut feeling about an idea? If so, congratulations, you are one-third of the way there! You have already accomplished step one of three.

Step 1 Feel It?

Congratulations! You have a strong feeling on a business idea and you are ready to take the call to action. Just fill out the information on the Break Equation Incubator page online and submit for consideration.

Step 2 See It?

If we select your Breaking Profile, our team of Break Advisors will contact you to complete a Break Audit. Think of it as a business idea overview. It will help to bring your vision and passion to life by showing a comprehensive roadmap of how that dream can become a reality.

Step 3 Do It?

Based on our consultative process in step two, we will collectively determine the resources needed to put that comprehensive roadmap into action. Using our proprietary network of resources available through our Break Advisors, we will work with you to agree on the implementation plan and then, simply, do it – together.

For more information on how the Break Equation Incubator process works or to learn how to join our team of Break Advisors, please visit us online at www.TheBreakEquation.com.

We hope these tools can help to bring your business idea and vision to reality. After all, that is the vision of *The Break Equation*.

CPSIA information can be obtained at www.ICGtesting.com
Printed in the USA
BVOW020200150911

271246BV00004B/2/P